The Crystal-Barkley
GUIDE TO
TAKING
CHARGE
OF
YOUR
CAREER

The Crystal-Barkley

GUIDE TO

TAKING CHARGE OF YOUR CAREER

by Nella Barkley
and Eric Sandburg

WORKMAN PUBLISHING • NEW YORK

Library of Congress Cataloging-in-Publication Data

Barkley, Nella
  The Crystal-Barkley guide to taking charge of your career / by Nella
Barkley and Eric Sandburg.
    p. cm.
Includes index.
ISBN 1-56305-495-7
1. Vocational guidance—United States. I. Sandburg, Eric.
II. Title.
HF5382.5.U5B295   1995
331.7'02—dc20   95-105
                    CIP

Cover and book illustrations by Sam Gross
Cover design by Paul Gamarello
Interior design by Rebecca Bazell with Natsumi Uda

Workman books are available at special discount when purchased in bulk for
special premiums and sales promotions as well as for fund-raising or
educational use. Special editions or book excerpts also can be created to
specification. For details, contact the Special Sales Director at the address
below.

Workman Publishing Company, Inc.
708 Broadway
New York, NY 10003-9555

Manufactured in the United States of America

First Printing January 1996
10 9 8 7 6 5 4 3 2 1

TO JOHN CURRY CRYSTAL,
WHO CREATED IN HIS OWN LIFE AND TEACHINGS
THE PROCESS AT THE HEART OF THIS BOOK,
WHICH IS OUR LIFESAVER

ACKNOWLEDGMENTS

Our first thanks go to John Crystal, whose remarkable capacity to see the truth in his own life and work enabled him to build the self-actualizing process that we now pass on to you. He taught Nella the secrets and subtleties that underlie the many layers of the process and together they built the Crystal-Barkley Corporation, ensuring that his concepts and practices will continue to develop and be available to a general public.

John's mind was like a room that, when you entered and lingered in it, revealed all the basics for living an extraordinary life. Indeed, his legacy is very much alive in the many thousands of people who use the Crystal-Barkley process to continually transform and redefine their lives. Again we thank you, John, for conveying the possibility of such richness to us.

We shall forever be in debt to Josleen Wilson, who in an exhaustive series of edits and re-edits helped us to translate the process into the printed word. She understands Crystal-Barkley's mission inside out and has in fact become our dear friend and partner in it, but without losing her perspective. Her craft and her dedication are remarkable.

All of our colleagues at Crystal-Barkley contributed in important ways, one of them being simply encouraging us to stay with it. Grace Broad, treasurer; Marjorie Long, senior consultant; Cliff Oblinger, consultant and corporate programs officer; Linda Yan, office manager; and Jeff Goodman, our consultant in Los Angeles are due special mention, for each in his or her way provided inspiration and a shoulder to lean on.

Margot Herrera, our editor at Workman Publishing, stuck by us through thick and thin and we are grateful to her for trying to see things in a different way when it would have been much easier not to. And we are grateful as well to Barbara Lowenstein, our agent, who kept us on track and was always ready to expedite matters.

Our biggest debt is to our families. It is not easy to put up with authors who are also running business enterprises. Penny Sandburg, in this regard proved more than just a loving wife; she was also a help-mate in a most professional sense. Nella's husband, Rufus, her three children—Rufus, Miles, and Nella and their growing families provided havens of diversion, warmth, and love.

And finally, we thank the Crystal-Barkley clients and those who have used our Career Design software, so many of whom have taken the trouble to stay in touch with us over the years, furnishing us with rich stories that prove the process works. They urge us to reach out in new ways so that even more individuals and organizations will have access to its benefits, and they are major figures in this piece of work.

CONTENTS

INTRODUCTION The Crystal-Barkley Advantage xi

Part One • WHO AM I?
Determining your skills, attributes, and values

1. Discovering Who You Are 1
2. Telling Your Life Stories 9
3. Defining Skills 19
4. Organizing Your Skills 25
5. Talking About Yourself 35
6. Uncovering Values 45

Part Two • WHERE AM I GOING?
Uncovering your interests and goals

7. What Do You Want Out of Life? 63
8. Interests and Fascinations 69
9. Finding Direction 75
10. Determining Your Goals 83

Part Three • HOW DO I GET THERE?
Landing the job

11. Assembling a Plan of Action 93
12. Making a Survey Plan 99
13. Effective Introductions 109
14. More About Surveying 117
15. Deciding Where You Want to Work 131
16. From Surveys to Proposals 143
17. Negotiating the Relationship 155
18. Long-term Survival and Satisfaction 165

APPENDICES

APPENDIX A Tips on Getting (and Staying) Organized . . 177
APPENDIX B How to Handle the Standard Interview . . . 181
APPENDIX C From Resumes to Proposals 199
INDEX 209

THE CRYSTAL-BARKLEY ADVANTAGE

Finding work that you love may seem a fantasy of wishful thinking in today's world. This book will show you how to use the Crystal-Barkley process to turn that fantasy into your most practical survival tool. Whether you are looking for work or thinking about changing jobs, feeling that you're in the wrong field entirely or trying to get a first toehold in the job market, you can put the same proven methods to work to ensure your prosperity and satisfaction. Whatever your individual circumstance, you are like many people struggling with the dilemma of finding rewarding, well-paying work that you enjoy and that enhances your personal life. Don't let today's downsizings and sweeping management innovations fool you into believing that good work, leading to a good life, is a remote possibility.

The image of the job market projected by the media can be so unnerving as to suggest that a working-age adult is in perpetual danger of being unemployed. And it's true that many organizations are trimming back to a core staff, where key employees remain with the company, and what they don't handle—from new-product development to plant maintenance to employee training—is outsourced.

For corporations, the goal of downsizing and outsourcing is to increase profits while maintaining, and even increasing, production and services. Thus, the employees that remain are working longer, more intense hours. Many find themselves being consumed by their jobs and constantly working overtime simply to keep pace. For them, and for millions of the unemployed or the about-to-be-unemployed, the issue of liking one's job is subordinate to having a job at all.

And yet, settling for work you feel "lucky" to get, or somehow making the best of an unsatisfactory job you have, can be the most dangerous course you can follow, and is precisely what you shouldn't do. We are in an era where people are being paid for performance. Those who slog along unhappily, especially in jobs that poorly match their interests and talents, seldom deliver top-quality work and will be among the first to go in a cutback.

Is it possible to find a dream job in such an inhospitable environment? Absolutely yes. But it requires a new way of thinking. The old way—sending out a resume and going on random interviews—was never especially brilliant. Today, it is completely ineffective. Consider this scenario: You prepare a resume listing your job titles and responsibilities in established organizations; then through an employment agency or on your own, you mail out resumes to well-known companies. The problem is that these organizations are often trying to eliminate the very same jobs that you have listed on your resume.

Similarly, identifying growth industries, and trying to fit yourself into them also produces poor results. "Growth trends" are notoriously unreliable. Trying to redefine yourself to fit a particular trend means that when more changes occur, you will have to redefine yourself all over again.

However, some of the changes taking place in business offer real opportunities to those who know how to go after them. Newly retooled organizations recognize and reward individual achievement. Even downsized organizations are hiring those who share their visions of new products, services, and marketing strategies. Thousands of new or smaller organizations are also looking for key employees to help their businesses grow.

Self-employment offers huge new opportunities for the right people. In a real sense, self-employed consultants achieve a new kind of security. Working for several different organizations spreads the sources of income and provides a breadth of experience sure to make them current in their fields. Consultants also become masters at marketing themselves and their specialty skills, and adept at forming new work associations with a variety of individuals and organizations. As a result, they are more confident about their ability to earn a good living, regardless of the changes in the job market.

To take advantage of new opportunities requires a new attitude and a new approach to scoping out a career. In the contemporary workplace, you must use your talents in ways that produce profit and satisfaction for yourself and others.

There *is* a new, best way of finding satisfying, joyful employment, and it begins with getting in touch with your own interests, values, and passions—*before* looking for a job. *This is true if you're a 21-year-old college graduate with an English degree, a 50-year-old laid-off telecommunications worker, or a machinist whose skills seem no longer needed.* And it's true whether you are going for an established staff position, creating a new job within an organization, or entering the unknown territory of self-employment.

Fine, you say. But what if I don't have a particular passion for work? What if I'm not even sure what kind of work I want to do? Or perhaps you do have an idea, but you don't think it could ever turn into a profitable occupation. It is not always easy to convince people to rethink their own enthusiasms—especially when they have already invested years in a particular field, or are loaded with financial obligations, or both.

Most of us have been thoroughly conditioned to believe that work is something other than what we'd like to be doing. From childhood on we get approval for doing what our parents, teachers, or peers expect of us. By the time we are adults, we no longer trust our own feelings and ideas.

But we will guarantee you right now, that you have definite, specific "callings" about which you can feel passionately and for which you are ideally suited. Even if you cannot name them at this moment, discovering and putting your true callings to work is the most practical step you can take toward a fulfilling and genuinely successful life.

How Crystal-Barkley Can Help

The *Crystal-Barkley Guide to Taking Charge of Your Career* offers a complete career-planning system that begins with finding out what you really want to be doing and takes you all the way to landing a job you love, and beyond. This innovative approach was pioneered by John C. Crystal who, with Nella Barkley, founded the New York-based Crystal-Barkley Corporation in 1981.

Constantly updated and refined, their unique career-planning method has been taught successfully to thousands of people who attend five-day marathon courses during which they participate in scores of activities to reveal hidden talents, desires, values, and interests.

Participants discover a personal sense of direction and develop market-research skills that end up giving them choices among several different employment situations. The coursework is followed by one-on-one consultations, in which all clients are coached in how to refine and carry out individual plans of action which match their lively bundle of attributes to the needs of employers.

This process has shown extraordinary results with thousands of people in hundreds of different careers, including business managers, line workers, artists of every kind, and entrepreneurs in every field. Surveys of individuals using the Crystal-Barkley process consistently show that more than 80 percent increased their satisfaction with their life and work or both. One survey that was conducted by an independent researcher from Columbia University showed this to be 89 percent.

In this book we have simplified the intensive five-day course into an accessible master program that invites you to complete the full process in record time. Think of the book itself as a friendly coach whom you are going to have around from now on; you will work with this coach in a concentrated way for the next few weeks, and then your visits will come on an as-needed basis. You will always have your coach available any time you feel stuck, or when you need to regain your perspective.

The Crystal-Barkley method is a fully integrated system that begins with *you*. It acknowledges the conditions of the present job market, but it is not driven by it. Every step in the program leads to the next, and all are eventually tied together into one interconnected piece. If you follow the steps sequentially, they will lead you to not just one but, we expect, a number of realistic work possibilities.

To help clarify the method you are about to learn and bring it to life, we include many anecdotes of how our clients have approached the same activities as you will. And to give you a sense of how the program works as a whole, we follow the job searches of two clients, David and Elizabeth, whom we will introduce a little later.

The Crystal-Barkley process is formed around three questions:

Who am I?

Surprising as it may sound, the first step to finding a great job is to *know yourself*. People looking for the right jobs amid fierce competition must first systematically define their personal skills and values. Our definition of skills is much broader than the one which might traditionally come to mind. When you learn the full range of your skills, you will begin to feel a confidence you have not experienced before.

Where am I going?

Uncovering your interests and motivations creates a magnetic pull toward specific work. Skills, interests, and values are eventually combined into an integrated personal "goals statement" that will guide your job search and decision-making. This newfound sense of mission represented in your goals statement will give you a zest for living that will make you very attractive to others.

How do I get there?

Once you have answered the first two questions, you can synthesize the results of your activities into a clear plan of action that will keep you headed where you want to be going for the rest of your life. Your challenge now is to prove to prospective employers—through powerful oral and written presentations—that you can solve problems, create products, and bring in revenue. Once you understand how to connect your skills and interests to an employer's needs, you will have grasped the secret of making yourself indispensable.

CONSIDERING SELF-EMPLOYMENT?

If you are considering starting your own business or working independently, you will want to work through this book with equal thoroughness. The self-marketing skills you'll learn work whether you are seeking a salaried position or you are your own employer, with clients who pay you for your goods or services. Therefore, whenever we say "job" we mean traditional jobs, freelance work, consultancy, or your own business. The process is exactly the same. In fact, the steps in this book may be even more important for you to take if you are considering going out on your own in view of the large numbers of failures among business start-ups. The failures are usually due to inadequate analysis and planning at the start of the venture.

How to Use This Book

The Crystal-Barkley process utilizes a series of personal exercises and activities that will help you determine what motivates and drives you. These activities may seem deceptively simple, and you will have fun with them. But in fact, each leads to complex, multilayered information, and most people recognize that they are being affected on a profound level. That is a natural part of the process. Also, bear in mind that the Crystal-Barkley method is an integrated process and all the pieces work together. For this reason, even if a chapter or a particular exercise doesn't seem pertinent to you, work through it anyway.

Like the full Crystal-Barkley course, this book requires an investment of time and effort to get the desired results. You should expect to take three to six weeks learning and working with the process. The advantage is that you can work at your own pace wherever you happen to be. Beyond your own commitment, the only tools you'll need are an open mind, a pencil, and a notebook (or a computer).

You will see how this all works out as you follow two former clients through their experiences. Elizabeth and David are real people who have shared their lives and their experiences fully here. Only their names and most identifiable locations have been changed to protect their privacy.

Elizabeth

Elizabeth grew up in the Northeast. Her mother was a secretary and her father was a manager at a large film manufacturing company. Elizabeth graduated from college with a BA in medieval history and English. After graduation, however, she felt as though she had wasted her time in school. There didn't seem to be much call for medieval scholars on the job market. She moved to New York and got a job working as an editorial assistant in a publishing firm that specialized in law books. She did baby-sitting on the side to supplement her salary, and in her spare time volunteered at a local hospital. Elizabeth didn't find her work very challenging, so she signed up for a night course in interior design, thinking she might like to pursue this as a career.

Her interest waned. Going to school at night was a strain, and she found she didn't enjoy the company of the other students. "I thought, if these are the kind of people I'll be working with as an interior designer, I don't want to be in this business." She quit the course. She also switched jobs, moving over to a pharmaceutical company's in-house publication for employees.

Elizabeth saved every dollar she could and eventually quit this job to hike and bike around Europe. When her money ran out she returned home and, after working at a couple of interim jobs, on a whim answered a newspaper ad for a "freelance comedy writer."

It seemed like a wild card, but people had always said she had a "flair" with words and a good sense of humor. Since childhood, Elizabeth had loved show business, although she never thought of these interests in terms of work. She got the writing job, which turned out to be contributing humor bits for greeting cards and gift booklets.

Although she enjoyed the work, she thought she'd better look for steadier employment. This time, she landed an entry-level spot writing catalog copy in the promotion department of another publishing company. Now she was writing every day, and she discovered she was good at it. She also took a course in screenwriting, thinking she might pursue a career as a writer.

Elizabeth spent nearly four years at the publishing company, and then, tired of work that had become boring to her, quit and started looking for freelance work. She continued to dabble in screenwriting, but never succeeded in completing a script. However, she quickly picked up editorial work from women's magazines, and became something of an expert on women's health and fitness. She was also hired to do research and writing assignments for other writers and editors working on major health books. She discovered that the more she presented herself as a writer, the more work she got.

This felt good at first because it made her feel like a professional and helped her develop a disciplined attitude toward her craft. Elizabeth learned how to deliver a variety of jobs on time and in reasonably good shape. She continued to get assignments, but they soon grew repetitive.

Then one day she got what looked like a break: through a friend in publishing she was hired to write the text for an illustrated show-business biography. The money wasn't great, and the deadline didn't allow for much creativity, but Elizabeth delivered a workmanlike manuscript, on time. She followed this project with two more celebrity biographies for the same publisher.

The biographies did fairly well, but little money wound up in Elizabeth's pocket. She was learning that it was very hard to make a significant income from writing. She continued accepting women's magazine assignments. But the work got less interesting and, as her cost of living went up, her income stayed just about the same. At this point, Elizabeth thought she had gone as far as she could go.

When we asked her what kind of writing she would like to be doing, she said she had no specific writing goals. "I feel stranded," she said. "I'm barely getting along financially, and it's the same old thing, over and over. And I don't feel motivated to do anything else."

David

David was the second child of a well-to-do family living in an attractive suburb north of Chicago. His father, a stockbroker, commuted into the city; his mother had given up her work as an illustrator shortly before David's older brother was born. David was born two years later, and a sister came along four years after that. Theirs was a congenial family with lots of backyard barbecues and Little League in the summer, skating in the winter, and family vacations by car.

At home, talk around the dinner table was about financial markets. All the children had savings and checking accounts, and by the time they were in their teens they were receiving regular investment lessons and had begun to buy a few stocks with the gift monies and earnings from odd jobs. In fact, this exercise became quite competitive.

Unlike others in the family, David was a reader. He consumed stories about adventure and survival and insisted on going to a camp that taught wilderness survival. He kept the family entertained with stories of his days in the wild. Both parents were proud of him, although they didn't quite understand his interests.

The children had attended excellent public schools and when it came time for high school, the boys were sent to Vermont to a prep school that was their father's alma mater, and the girls went to a private school near home. Though David wished to stay at home for high school, it never really occurred to him that it would be possible and, besides, doing so would have disappointed his father.

David did well in school and earned a reputation as an excellent speaker and debater. He went on to Yale, where he majored in economics and minored in psychology. Summers he worked as a camp counselor or wilderness guide, and after graduation he took a management training position with a growing Chicago bank. By this time, his older brother had been asked to join the same brokerage firm in which his father was now a partner.

The bank treated David well and he liked the people he worked with. He especially enjoyed training new employees. David worked his way up as a lending officer, all the while continuing to study the behavior and career paths of the senior officers. He applied and was accepted by the business school at the University of Virginia, was granted a leave of absence and helped with tuition by the bank. While in Virginia he met and married the daughter of one of his favorite professors. The marriage didn't survive the move back to Chicago.

David's career progressed rapidly after he returned to the bank. He was transferred to Texas, then received an offer to join a California bank, where he quickly moved up in the mergers-and-acquisitions department and became the right-hand man to the bank's president and CEO. In this position, David showed himself to be an astute judge of people. Much of his responsibility involved correctly judging the motivations of those in his own bank and in target organizations. The president came to depend on him. These were heady days for David, as he was working near the center of power and feeling that he could exercise power himself. David was analytical and systematic, loved giving polished presentations, and enjoyed a fair amount of autonomy.

In his little time off from work, David went hiking, explored Los Angeles restaurants, and even took an advanced Dale Carnegie course, where he met a lovely woman who was an investment counselor for a competing bank. They married two years later.

Then the inevitable happened. David's bank became a takeover target itself. In the ensuing deal the president, David's mentor, was kicked upstairs and lost his power. Now the fun and challenges were over for David. He lost his autonomy, his champion, and his influence. David decided to leave.

Although the experience had left him with highly developed financial, analytical, negotiation, and presentation skills, David realized—when he allowed himself to think about it—that banking itself didn't mean a thing to him. He concluded that he didn't want to live the rest of his life doing excellent work for an end that wasn't important to him. But what to do?

David decided to give himself a one-year sabbatical to explore his unanswered questions.

Part One

WHO AM I?

*Determining your
skills, attributes, and values*

Discovering Who You Are

WHAT BETTER PLACE to begin than with the unique combination of skills and talents that comprise you? You may not fully appreciate it yet, but you have a distinctive approach to life derived from your personality. Like most people, however, you probably have a limited view of yourself. Somehow, in the process of adapting ourselves to the world and to other people, we lose sight of many of our natural gifts. The problem is, until you fill out the picture, other people—including the people you may want to hire you, buy something from you, or perhaps become your business partners—will have a limited view too. The more you can project the unique person you are, the greater your chance of finding work that excites you.

COMING UP

The real you!

☞ Discover that there's far more to you than you may have realized.

☞ Learn that you have many different, very useful skills.

☞ Identify the particular types of skills you have.

☞ Enhance your understanding of the nature of skills.

☞ Broaden your definition of skills.

Everyone wants to have a satisfying life, and there *is* a formula for getting one. The first set of steps involves uncovering your particular way of doing things: your skills, talents, and aptitudes (for the purpose of simplicity, all of which we'll call skills). Thoroughly understanding these skills means you can put them to work for yourself and others in ways that feel natural and good. You don't have to wait for the weekends to enjoy life. If you use your best skills on the job, you'll get pleasure and satisfaction during the work week too.

Discovering Your Skills

First, take a look at Appendix A, page 177, for some tips on getting organized before starting the Crystal-Barkley process. Then get out your notebook or computer and call the first section: **Who am I?** Label the first tab: *Discovering Skills.* Make a heading: "First Look at Skills."

NEED CLUES?

- Include physical skills as well as intellectual ones.
- Even if you think a skill is unimportant, list it.
- Consider skills you use to motivate yourself and others.
- How about the skills you use around home?
- What skills did or do you use in school?

- What skills do you call upon in your paid or unpaid work? In your recreational activities?
- Think of skills you learned and used when you were very young (skating, memorizing).
- What do you do every day or week that someone from outside your community might not know how to do?

Now, write down every skill you think you have. If you get stuck, check out the "Need Clues?" box above.

To help discover your full range of skills, try thinking about them in groups. Skills tend to fall into three main categories: basic, specific, and personality.

Basic Skills

Basic, or functional, skills, like reading and writing, are the tools of day-to-day living. They are often learned early in life and by the time you grow up are taken for granted.

Although everyone routinely uses basic skills, they are never trivial. Take a look at how Elizabeth, a 35-year-old writer, and David, a 37-year-old former banker, started their lists of basic skills, and then create your own. (For an introduction to Elizabeth and David, see page xvi.)

ELIZABETH'S BASIC SKILLS
- Driving a car (stick shift)
- Balancing a checkbook
- Adhering to a schedule
- Following instructions
- Hanging pictures by sight
- Playing cards
- Good memory
- Riding a bike
- Sewing from patterns

DAVID'S BASIC SKILLS
- Expressing opinions logically
- Wilderness hiking
- Making lists and prioritizing
- Giving good directions
- Reading road maps
- Good with numbers
- Retaining what I read

Specific Skills

Specific skills are acquired in school or on the job. These are often complicated—like computer programming or editing—and usually have a language of their own. Every job and life experience develops a number of such skills: Elizabeth and David both came up with specific skills associated with their present work but were surprised to find they also had many other specific skills they had forgotten about.

Make your list of specific skills as long as you can. Bear in mind that a specific skill doesn't have to be work-related to carry a high level of competency. As you'll see below, Elizabeth and David both included skills derived from recreational experiences in their youth.

ELIZABETH'S
SPECIFIC SKILLS

- Typing fast
- Researching using library and computer networks
- Editing and producing print media
- Doing interviews
- Analyzing technical medical articles
- Comedy writing
- Bartending
- Planning complex foreign travel
- Gourmet cooking

DAVID'S SPECIFIC SKILLS

- Prudent financial management
- Understanding legal documents
- Facility with numbers
- Technical knowledge of financial markets
- Evaluating credit risks
- Public speaking
- Excellent debating and speaking skills
- Mountain climbing
- Expert knowledge of first aid
- Playing golf

NEED CLUES?

- Have you learned specific skills in training courses or at school?
- How about on-the-job training? Off-the-job?
- Any correspondence courses or night courses?

- Have you taken lessons to improve your proficiency in sports? Music? Art? Cooking?
- Has anyone ever asked you, "How did you learn to do that?" What skill was involved?

Personality Skills

Personality skills describe the ways you behave or adapt to your environment. If people describe you as enthusiastic, careful, persistent, or independent, they are describing a personality skill. These are usually innate characteristics—like cheerfulness or determination—that remain the same over time. Including this category broadens your definition of skills and also adds dimension and color to your self-portrait.

It's not always easy to define our own personalities because we often feel differently on the inside from the way we present ourselves on the outside. A person who feels shy, for example, may not appear shy to other people. You can practice identifying personality skills by considering how you might describe someone else. Think of someone you know

Personality skills are the reason most people get hired—or fired.

well; then quickly name 10 personality traits you would use to describe the person. The traits are probably different from your own, but thinking about another person helps you get the idea. Also take a look at a few of the personality skills that David and Elizabeth listed. Then create a list that includes what you believe to be your own personality skills. Don't hold back.

ELIZABETH'S PERSONALITY SKILLS	DAVID'S PERSONALITY SKILLS
• Honest	• Sincere
• Flexible	• Highly organized
• Logical	• Persistent
• Tactful	• Ebullient
• Generous	• Conceptual thinker
• Intuitive	• Long-range perspective
• Introspective	• Confident
• Open-minded	• Creative
• Sentimental	• Self-motivated
• Stylish	• Overachieving
• Liberal	• Dynamic
• Intelligent	• Innate common sense
• Articulate	• Detail-oriented

NEED CLUES?

- What qualities do you like best in people? Do you possess any of these?
- How do you think your friends and colleagues would describe you?
- When people praise you, they are often describing personality skills. Try to remember how you have been complimented in the past.
- Forget modesty. What's the best thing that anybody ever said about you?

We are all loaded with personality skills, and they are all *good*. The trick is to find a work situation where your particular personality skills are appreciated. In the right environment, any personality skill can be an asset. Being a "loner," for example, comes in handy in forestry or scientific research where the ability to work solo is essential. Being a "nit-picker" is a great quality if you are in quality control, proofreading, research, and many other types of work.

The way we see it, any aspect of your personality is a skill when it helps you become productive and enthusiastic. Assume you know that you work (or play) best with one or two other people. Is this a skill? Definitely. Working well in small groups is an asset in many jobs.

Suppose you can tolerate quite a bit of messiness and confusion. Is this a skill? It can be if you work in a freewheeling company. Tolerating a certain amount of chaos (and even thriving in it) implies that you are flexible and can adjust to the habits of co-workers.

It's never enough to have only the specific skills needed to get the job done. Having the right personality for the job gives you that competitive edge. It is also the quickest, most effective path to raises, promotions, and recognition, because your bosses will relate to you and like you. When they feel comfortable having you around, you are likely to stay.

Digging Deeper

Even if you think you've listed all your abilities, talents, and attributes, you have more to come. At the top of a new page write "More Skills." As you look at the list below, challenge yourself to find as many skills in each category as possible. Be super-generous to yourself. Consider your:

- Interests
- Hobbies (past and present)
- Achievements
- Talents and other natural abilities
- Wishes and desires
- "Tropisms"—things that attract or repel you
- Preferred environments— the types of settings that feel best to you

What skills do you associate with those categories? Suppose you remember spending long afternoons building model airplanes? What skills are apparent? Patience, attention to detail, fascination with aircraft, persistence, and careful planning are all readily transferable to work for pay.

Let's look at how a few other people's hobbies and interests have shaped their careers:

■ "Fascination with Romanesque churches" led one woman into teaching art history.

■ "Putting together all manner of models on a very fine scale" was eventually put to work creating architectural models and shadowbox museum exhibits.

■ "Loving hiking under extremely rugged conditions" resulted in one man testing outdoor camping equipment and eventually becoming CEO of a camping equipment manufacturing company.

To Sum Up

Skills of all types and at various levels of competency are what you have to offer an employer, partner, or client. Don't worry about placing your skills in exactly the right category. The categories are merely a convenience to help you organize your thoughts and encourage you to include every possibility. Later you'll have time to decide which skills are most important to you. For now, don't rule out anything. Fill as many sheets of paper or type in as much as you can. You'll likely be able to put this broader vision of yourself to work right away. Your

Be yourself. No one else is qualified.

first steps in discovering who you are will probably make you sit up and take notice of yourself in ways that will encourage others to notice too.

Telling Your Life Stories

I N THIS CHAPTER, we ask you to tell stories about times when you enjoyed yourself or felt a sense of achievement. Telling such stories will reveal much more about you and your skills than you were able to put down in your lists. What we call "Life Stories" are vignettes of happy, rewarding, or meaningful moments that stand out in your mind. For example, one person wrote a story about going to the seashore with her dad when she was a small child. Someone else described the time his boss unexpectedly asked him to fill in as a convention panelist.

Stories don't have to be about work. Do you remember feeling good about something you were doing? Start there.

COMING UP

How your past can help determine your future.

☞ First, learn from other people's stories about how to tell your own.

☞ Rediscover patterns of interests and activities that hold special meaning for you.

☞ Find out how to tell your stories in ways that reveal hidden talents.

No one else could describe this experience in quite the same way, because no one else knows how you actually felt about a particular event, even if someone else was there with you at the time. So trust your instincts when you start to tell your stories.

Hidden Talents

One important reward of telling your life stories is that as you recall incidents from your past forgotten skills and strengths emerge and you begin to see yourself in a fresh light. Many of us find it surprising to realize that we can capitalize on skills that came naturally to us as children. The trouble is that many of these skills fall into disuse because we lose touch with them while doing jobs that use lesser strengths. Thinking back on childhood activities reminds us of the skills that come easily to us. And recognizing our natural skills has a lot to do with knowing how to create rewarding work.

You are the only one capable of being an expert on you.

For example, the founder and president of Mrs. Fields Cookies says that she started the multimillion-dollar company that bears her name in 1978—as an unemployed 20-year-old with only a high school diploma and no recognizable skills—because the one thing she always loved doing, even as a child, was baking cookies for her friends and family.

S.GROSS

"He learned to ride at a very early age."

When you're not accustomed to recognizing your skills, it helps to look at other people's experiences. Take a look at one of Elizabeth's stories. After you have had a chance to pinpoint the skills evident in her story, you will be in a better position to work on your own.

Elizabeth's Medieval Summer

One summer during college I applied for a job at the Cloisters, the New York museum built in the style of a medieval monastery, that specializes in medieval art. Every summer the museum sponsored a camp that was attended by inner-city kids who learned about knights and medieval arts and crafts four days a week. At the end of the session, they demonstrated what they'd learned in a special medieval festival.

A friend went up there with me and while I was being interviewed for the job, she walked around the grounds. Afterward I took her into one of the tapestry rooms to see the big hangings and told her all the stories they depicted, which I knew by heart. When I turned around, about 15 people were standing there, listening. They thought I was a docent. Medieval art is just one of those things I'm able to talk about naturally.

I got the job and worked all summer with kids from the neighborhood, making banners and costumes, weaving baskets, and learning quasi-medieval skills for the festival. One day we ran out of things to do and I dragged a few of the kids into the museum and showed them some of the art. I vividly remember one kid looking at a painting called *The Three Temptations of Christ.* He looked at me and said, "What's going on in this picture?" I told him about it. Then he said, "And what's Jesus doing here?"

I explained that he was saying, "Get thee behind me, Satan." Again, when we walked away I found a group of people following us, staring at me as if I worked there as a curator.

In your notebook or computer, write down the skills you can find in Elizabeth's story. Label this sheet "Elizabeth's Skills."

NEED CLUES?

- Remember, personality traits count as skills. What kind of personality do you suppose Elizabeth had that generated so much interest from other people?
- What natural abilities or talents stand out? What does Elizabeth seem to be doing with very little effort?
- Some skills come from the overall sense of the story, rather than a specific thing she did. Think of the impression that the story makes.
- If you get stuck, reread the story. Write down any thought that occurs to you. You cannot overdo it. The more skills, the better.

- You may find that similar skills are revealed in several places. Describe each a little differently.
- Action verbs are big clues. Look for words such as *coaching, leading, planning.*
- Think of the personal qualities and strengths Elizabeth displayed by working with disadvantaged children.
- What specific skills or techniques do you suppose she used to get cooperation from the children?
- What skills are revealed by specific activities?
- Push yourself as far as you can before you continue reading below to discover some skills we found in Elizabeth's story.

A Few of Elizabeth's Skills

Here are some of the skills we found in Elizabeth's story.

- Telling an interesting story
- Getting along easily with others
- Effectively gathering information
- Loving history ever since childhood
- Being fascinated by medieval art
- Feeling strongly motivated to learn and share knowledge
- Independently following own interests
- Having a good memory for historical and visual detail
- Easily engaging a group with historical presentations
- Relating well to children from various backgrounds
- Conveying arcane information in an interesting manner
- Exercising appropriate discipline with young children who are unaccustomed to it

- Organizing lesson plans
- Laying out designs attractively
- Teaching basic sewing
- Possessing good hand-eye coordination
- Weaving baskets in medieval designs
- Helping others to imagine another era
- Integrating activities with those of other staff
- Being a storehouse of medieval anecdotes
- Unselfconsciously conveying interests, even to strangers
- Interpreting historical data for both sophisticated and unschooled audiences
- Successfully presenting herself to museum administrators

To us, the entire episode suggests that Elizabeth had a passion that she pursued joyfully and independently. She showed strong teaching and organizational skills, as long as the subject related to her interest. It is also obvious that she has considerable depth of knowledge of the medieval period.

What Stories Should You Tell?

When it comes to writing your own life stories, it helps to organize some thoughts ahead of time. Think back on moments that you remember vividly—times when you felt challenged, enjoyed doing something, or had an adventure. They can be from any period in your life and they don't all have to be happy memories.

One person wrote a life story about organizing his department's holiday toy-collection drive and how successfully it turned out. Another recalled the troubles he had in the first week after moving to Boston from a small Midwestern town. Somebody else wrote a story about starting a city garden; another about spending time with his grandparents. No matter what you write about, it helps to think of each story as a chapter.

Start a new tab in your notebook, and label it: *Life Stories*. As a fresh heading, write: "Chapters." Give each story that you plan to tell a title that's fun and evocative for you ("Sand Between My Toes," "The Country Bumpkin," "Cabbages and Cobblestones," "On the Road to Montreal," "My Tie to Reality"—whatever works for you). These stories will become chapters in a book about *you*.

Here are the titles that David gave to his life stories:

- "Little League Champ"
- "Uncle Rich"
- "Overdrawn"
- "The Lost Steaks"
- "Out of Sight"
- "Dr. Psych"
- "Alice"
- "Passing It On"
- "The Texas Mergers and Acquisitions Scene"
- "Life Next to Power"
- "Time Out"
- "Behind the Microphone"

Stories can be about a particular time in your life, an activity or event that meant a lot to you, a challenge you faced, or a place you visited. Sequence doesn't matter—your chapters might be chronological or organized by categories such as activities, leisure, school, and/or work. The point is to have fun reliving them.

When you have a list of stories, look it over and put an asterisk next to the one you feel like telling first. (No, not the one you think is most important! Choose the story that you most enjoy remembering.)

NEED CLUES?

- Review old journals or diaries to recall significant moments in your life.
- Think of your life as chapters in a wonderful, personal book.
- Life stories are not diaries; they are descriptions of your actions at specific times of your life.
- Choose stories in which you were an active participant. A story about watching TV for relaxation doesn't tell much about your skills. But a story about watching television in order to analyze advertising techniques does tell something about you.
- Sometimes in writing one story, memories of another event will come to you. Make a note and create the other story later.
- Use humor; it gives you energy to tell the story.
- Be imaginative. Titles such as "Ruling the Roost" or "Coming Into My Own" are more interesting than "0 to 8 Years."

Writing Your Stories

Start each story on a new page, and plan to write for two or three pages. (You can talk into a tape recorder if you wish; talk for at least 10 minutes. If you record, make sure to flip the tab on the tape so it cannot be erased.) In addition:

■ As you tell the story, emphasize *how* you did something, not why (this is not a psychological document).

■ Describe how you felt about this activity.

■ Tell how you got along with other people in the story.

■ And tell what happened as a result of what you did.

Remembering *How* Tells It All

Saying "I won a tennis tournament when I was 12," is a conclusion; it does not describe *how* you won. A more revealing description is: "I won a tennis tournament by practicing a lot each day, by playing practice matches, by psyching myself up mentally before each match, and by figuring out my opponent's weaknesses." An even better one is:

> To win the tennis tournament I practiced at least one hour every day. I worked on drills until I was confident about each part of my game. I spent extra time working on the weak parts, especially my serve. Doing drills was sometimes boring and exhausting, but it got results. I also took every opportunity to watch other players in my group and analyze their games.
>
> On match days I arrived early, so I always had enough time to warm up and not feel rushed. During the match, it was easy to feel the pressure, so I would mentally control my thoughts to focus on each point, one stroke at a time. I would probe my opponent's game for weaknesses and mix up my shots to keep her off balance . . .

Remember, if something was a problem, *how* did you solve it? If you were unhappy about something, *how* did you cope with it? If something gave you a real sense of accomplishment, *how* did you make it happen? Reading one of David's life stories will give you the idea.

David's Wilderness Trek

The last year I went to camp I earned the highest level guide badge. I was 15 and had been going to Camp Tremount for four summers. I had eagerly looked forward to the solo trip that the most advanced campers took—it was the top achievement at the camp. But when the time came I felt a little scared underneath the excitement. I would have to spend three days and nights in the wilderness alone. I recall thinking, *Oh, well, no one—that I know of—has died on one of these yet.*

I packed my bedroll, tarp, and the meager supplies I was permitted. It would be cold at night so I carried a warm jacket. I had enough water for one day and some trail mix, but I was expected to find water and forage for most of my food. I carried a map, compass, journal, pen, flashlight, a large camp knife, canteen, tin cup, water purifying tablets, and frying pan (but no matches). All in all, it was a fairly light backpack.

Even now, reading back over the journal I kept, I can feel excitement well up in my throat. I was carried by van to the top of a ridge. My mission was to cross over to the neighboring ridge, then descend to the pickup point, where the Sheephorn and Campbell rivers met. At noon on the fourth day, I would be picked up by the van.

I was familiar with mountainous terrain, although I had never been to this exact place. I could make out the trail leading to the top of the opposite ridge. I calculated that if I reached the top by the second night, I could make it down to the pickup point on time. I was eager to get going but made myself take the time to compare the view with my map and plot a route that would minimize steep climbs. Then I took off, following old trails along the first ridge for the rest of that day.

I had expected to spend the night up on the ridge, but as it turned out I was already beginning to descend at nightfall; it was well past dinnertime, which I had completely forgotten. I ate a bit of trail mix and went to bed in a grassy hollow under the stars.

The next morning was sparkling and cold. I couldn't wait to get going to warm up and look for food. My water was almost gone and I thought I'd better save the trail mix for emergencies.

The huckleberries I found on the way down made a fabulous breakfast. I took some extra time to fill my cup and pan for later. I also found an interesting red berry, but I remembered it might be poisonous and avoided it, as I did the mushrooms I found later.

Coming upon a stream near the valley floor, I filled my canteen and made myself a snare (something I'd learned the previous summer) and succeeded in trapping a steelhead—taking too much time to do it. Still, I was pretty excited. I cleaned it, wrapped it grass and leaves, and packed it away in the middle of my bedroll for dinner. Then I took off up the next mountain and didn't stop again until it was almost dark.

I stripped bark husk and rubbed sticks together until I finally got a fire going. That fish, along with the huckleberries, made a gourmet dinner.

All was well until a thunderstorm blew up in the middle of the night. Rivulets of water streamed over the tarp and leaked into my bedroll, which cost me time the next day getting everything dried out. Fortunately, the morning sun was warm and bright. It was rough going and I was beginning to tire. I was also getting hungry, but the huckleberries saved me.

At nightfall on the last night a deer crossed my path and I wished for a bow and arrow. I settled for some wild onions and field greens that I had learned were okay, but I didn't feel so good afterward. Sleep restored me, and it was a good thing, for in the morning I could see bear tracks around my campground. I moved with greater speed than usual.

When I caught sight of the confluence of the two rivers below, I was elated and thought, *I can do it.* And I did.

A Quick Analysis

This story reveals a multitude of skills. Here are only a few that David spotted:

- Persisting in the face of physical and psychological challenges.
- Systematically and prudently laying out a survival plan.
- Showing considerable knowledge of wild flora and fauna.
- Showing resourcefulness in using materials at hand.

MORE CLUES

- The more details you tell about yourself, the more you will learn, so be generous in your storytelling.
- Visualize a chapter as though you were watching a movie; describe it simply, but in detail.

- Grammar and style are unimportant. Write freely and continuously. Tell the story your own way, without editing yourself.
- Concentrate on the *how* of what you did, not the why.

To Sum Up

Life stories are the foundation of the Crystal-Barkley process. They provide insight into how you do things, how you feel about doing them, and what results you get—information that only you can know. Telling them will be enjoyable if you do one or two at a time. After telling one story, read it through several times and identify the skills. This combination of writing the stories and identifying skills is so immediately gratifying and informative that most people feel enthusiastic about continuing the process. The more stories you tell, the more you will feel like telling. The more you

Your most important resource is yourself.

do, the more information you have to work with. Plan to spend at least a week telling stories and identifying skills. You should end up with 12 or more stories. Your effort now, at the beginning of the Career Design process, directly affects your ability to stand out in the job market when the time comes to choose the right job.

CHAPTER THREE

Defining Skills

B Y NOW WE hope you are starting to feel more like the unique person you are. Capturing your individuality should be ample reward for the time and trouble you are taking to tell life stories and identify your skills. The fact is, the more fully you identify your skills, the more useful they will be to you. You'll eventually use this information in presenting yourself to prospective employers, so it's vital that your description be complete and precise. This is no time to sell yourself short. That means pushing yourself even further toward a clear, even magnetic, description of your capacities.

COMING UP

An even more sophisticated way to describe yourself.

☞ Learn a three-part format to enhance skills identification.

☞ Apply this format to upgrade the skills you identified earlier.

☞ Access hidden skills with help from others.

If you're thinking, "Uh-oh, this is a lot of trouble. Maybe I'll just go along as I have been," consider this scenario:

One of our clients, Doreen, was making a pitch to the special-events manager of a major theme park. She wanted to plan tours for foreign visitors that would help them take full advantage of the the park. Her idea was to give the park a unique appeal over other tourist attractions.

The special-events manager asked, "How do you know you'll be able to do this?"

Doreen answered, "I know I'm good at planning."

"Planning what?" the manager asked.

"Planning exciting tours for groups of people, particularly people from other cultures."

"How do you know?"

Doreen answered, "Because I've done it before. I used to take foreign visitors around the campus when I was a senior in college. My groups always had a good time, and I was asked to take others. People of all ages were in the groups, not just prospective students."

"And did you do this anywhere else?"

Doreen fidgeted a bit, then said, "Yes, as a matter of fact, the Chamber of Commerce asked me to organize the visits of several Asian trade groups and one from the Netherlands. These were quite a challenge, but I had a great time doing it."

"Why didn't you tell me this straight out?"

Instead of making her interviewer pry it out of her, Doreen's first response would have been much more compelling if she had said, "For some time people have been telling me I have a special talent for organizing group tours for foreign visitors of all ages. I organized tours that were educational *and* entertaining for both my college and the Chamber of Commerce, and they came back asking for more." More important, Doreen could have gone into the discussion feeling confident, rather than defensive about her first assertion.

Preparation before interviews boosts confidence and helps you feel in control. And the best preparation you can have is a clear, in-depth knowledge of your skills.

Skills can be described in dozens of ways, but they should always include three elements: how well you did something, what you did, and in what context you did it.

HOW WELL	WHAT	WHERE—OR FOR WHAT PURPOSE
Usually an adverb or adjective that describes your special quality or attitude	An "ing" verb that tells exactly what you were doing	A word or phrase that gives the location or in some way puts the event in context

Think back to some of your one-word skills that you identified earlier. Perhaps you have something like "enthusiasm" on your list of personality skills. "Enthusiasm" is a wonderful quality, but unless you put it in context—what were you being enthusiastic about and where—it doesn't provide much information.

HOW WELL	WHAT	WHERE—OR FOR WHAT PURPOSE
Enthusiastically	Enlisting volunteers	To assist in building housing for the homeless

All the necessary descriptive elements are present in a convenient 1-2-3 sequence, although the order itself is unimportant. You might find it easier to begin the sentence with "What" or "Where." Your description could have read, "Enlisting volunteers enthusiastically to assist in building housing for the homeless." All of the elements are still there. The idea is to describe each of your skills in as complete a fashion as you can.

"What else does he do besides chase cars?"

NEED CLUES?

- Is the following a skill? "Having an excellent sense of timing." Yes, but it needs more context. Try: "Displaying an excellent sense of timing in my comedy routine (cooking gourmet meals, stock car racing)."
- For each skill or action, ask yourself these questions:
  - How good was I at doing this?
  - Where was I doing it?
  - What compliments did I receive?
  - What adverbs do the compliments suggest?
  - How did I feel while I was doing this?
  - Who else was involved?
- Why did I decide to this?
- Helpful adverbs: thoroughly, assertively, pleasantly, perceptively, responsibly, effectively, accurately, boldly, courageously, systematically, consistently, punctually, habitually, energetically, positively, competently, insightfully, compassionately, efficiently, quietly, kindly, persistently. (Check a thesaurus or synonym finder if you run out of words.)
- Don't forget descriptive phrases such as: "with great determination," "with foresight and planning," "with careful attention to detail."

Review all of the skills you have identified so far. Using the clues above, take the time to put each one in the three-part format and transfer each to a small card or piece of paper (about the size of a business card is perfect). From now on, write your skills on these cards.

Uncovering Skills With Others

Working with other people to help identify your skills is even more fun and more productive than doing it alone. Remember, identifying skills is always a positive exercise; it points out your strengths. Here's how to take advantage of the tremendous benefits of pinpointing skills with others:

1. Find one, two, or three friends who are also interested in learning about themselves. (The method works with strangers too, so don't hesitate to invite interested newcomers into your group.) Make sure that everyone working with you understands that this is an in-depth technique for revealing skills.

2. Before you get together, ask each person to write down one "life story," just as you have: a little vignette with an amusing name.

3. Each person should identify all the skills he or she can see in the story, writing each one on a separate skill card and putting a code on the back that identifies the story. One such code might read "GP" for "Salvaging the Garden Patch."

4. Get together with your friends in a quiet place where you can work together for at least an hour. Have on hand a good supply of cards or pieces of paper. (At the beginning, as a reminder, you might mark a few cards with "How Well," "What," and "Where.")

5. Get one person to volunteer to read his or her story aloud first. Let's say it's you. Read your story all the way through without stopping; then reread it, letting your friends ask questions. As you read your story, the others should jot down on the cards the skills they perceive.

Without the insight of others, we would have very small windows on ourselves.

A note about writing down the skills you perceive in others' stories: Write the skills in the first person, as if they were your own. While this may feel odd at first, when you present the skills to their owners, they will feel more like they truly possess them.

6. When everyone is finished writing, you read aloud the cards you yourself prepared. The next person then reads the skills he or she identified and hands the cards to you to keep. In turn, the rest of the participants do the same. Accept every skill card with thanks. If you can't see a particular skill yourself, you can ask the others how they spotted it. The magic of working with other people is that they can see attributes you don't. In the end, you are the final arbiter, but give yourself the benefit of their insights.

7. Mark the back of each skill card you receive with the code of the story it refers to so if you need to expand on it later, you know where you found it. Then have the next person read his or her story aloud and follow the same procedure.

In one session you will quickly see the advantage of working with other people in identifying skills. Others are often more accurate and more positive about our qualities than we are. In other words, most of us don't give ourselves enough credit for the things we do. You will separate yourself from the rank and file by means of your group's help.

There's another advantage to working with other people. Important life events are occasionally sad or disappointing, and may even represent times when you feel you failed. But these stories often contain valuable insights about your ability to cope with adversity. Sharing them with your group can give you an entirely new view of the experience. Your cohorts will pick up the positive aspects of a time in your life you might have otherwise considered wholly negative and give you a new slant on your skills. Always begin the skill identification process with happy memories, however; it's easier.

Establish a regular schedule for getting together with your friends to continue the process. With these meetings to look forward to, you won't get into a rut working alone.

To Sum Up

You have learned to identify skills in a manner that fully represents your capacities. Eventually you will accumulate a hundred or more skill cards from a dozen stories. You can continue telling stories and adding cards even as you go on to Parts Two and Three of this book. (If you get too far ahead of yourself, though, you may have to catch up on your skill cards before going on. The book will cue you if this is about to happen.)

Remember, when identifying skills, always accentuate the positive. Assets are the name of this game.

CHAPTER FOUR

Organizing Your Skills

B Y THIS TIME you may feel overwhelmed by all the things you've learned about yourself. You have numerous notebook entries and a pile of skill cards, but you might be asking what they all add up to. Or perhaps you're wondering how you will convey these skills to someone. Relax— you have already completed the critical preparation that will help you distinguish yourself when it comes time to propose your services to a potential employer. The degree of self-knowledge you possess at this point is rare in today's world; what you choose to say about yourself and how you present yourself in the future will have the weight of your conviction behind it. You may feel like our client Sharon who said, "I've met a whole new person— and she's wonderful!"

COMING UP

How to put a spotlight on your strongest skills.

☛ Learn how to organize your skill cards into groups called *skill clusters*.

☛ Refine these clusters until they feel solid and accurate.

☛ Name each cluster so that you capture its depth and intensity.

☛ Come away with a sense of your *super skills*, those skills that represent the things you enjoy doing most and are best at.

Organizing Your Skills Into Clusters

"Clustering" skill cards is a way to manage an overwhelming amount of personal information. Through the process itself, you will get an even clearer picture of your key strengths.

Set aside an evening or afternoon when no one is around. This means *no one;* the last thing you need is someone looking over your shoulder trying to match up your skills for you. In addition, clustering works best when:

- It's done alone.
- It's done quickly.
- It takes advantage of your *feelings* about your skills.

In this activity your intuition is more important than any intellectual analysis. We know you can't turn your mind off, but you can tap into the more intuitive, or emotional side of your mind.

BE SURE YOU'RE READY

Before you can take these steps you need to have completed stories about the significant time periods and activities in your life and to have identified the skills in each one. You should have *at least 12 stories* with 100 or more skill cards. The more stories and skill cards you have, the larger the window you will have on yourself.

Intuition invariably leads you to associate skills that work well together.

David spied an association among several of his skill cards. One read "Quickly preparing an easily understandable budget." His eye went next to a card that read "Talking comfortably to professional peers about their needs." Then to "Creatively and accurately preparing economic forecasts for companies being acquired." And then to "Being fascinated with numbers since childhood."

Only David knew whether or how well these attributes worked together. And he knew it (as you will) without ever thinking about it.

Getting Started

When you are ready to begin, turn off the telephone, put the dog out, turn on your favorite music, and find a big flat surface (the dining table, the floor, a bed).

Divide your skill cards into manageable stacks (30 to 50 each) and shuffle each pile as you would a deck of cards. Working with one stack at a time, place the cards on the flat surface, arranging them writing side up and facing in the same direction so you can read them easily.

Let your eyes roam over the cards, taking in the myriad skills which represent your various competencies. When the spirit moves you, pick up the first card you feel drawn to. Select another card; if it seems related to the first one, place them together. If not, put it by itself. Working quickly, pick up a card on every third or fourth beat of the music. (You're playing music for more than aesthetic reasons.) If a card fits into more than one cluster, make a duplicate. It's normal for some skills to fit into more than one group. Soon you will have several "clusters" of skill cards, each representing a functional area in which you have a high degree of competence.

> *There's more richness in the "average" person than geniuses would ever have the time to put to work.*

When you have several clusters with a few cards in each, pause to pick up and look through them. From each group, select one card that seems to say the most about the nature of that cluster and lay it on top. If you can't find a card that seems to sum up the group, take a blank card and, using a different color ink, write a temporary name for the cluster; lay the new card on top.

Pick up the tempo again and use all your skill cards, continuing to create new clusters and adding to those you've already begun.

When all of your skill cards have been used, you will have in front of you little piles that contain solid evidence of "who you are." Put a rubber band around each cluster of skill cards and set them aside. With your assets clear in your mind, you'll soon be ready to show them off.

A Clustering Practice

Below is a list of skills lifted from David's total stack of cards, before clustering. For a moment, put yourself in David's shoes.

■ Confidently presenting ideas before large audiences

■ Effectively questioning people I don't know while I'm traveling

■ Persistently perfecting speeches

- Tactfully calming down excited people
- Enthusiastically participating in a highly committed team
- Patiently helping others learn a new skill
- Naturally maintaining a sense of humor when challenged
- Successfully persuading others to accept another point of view
- Working on every detail of a presentation plan with great care
- Objectively weighing the pros and cons of work alternatives
- Accurately assessing an audience's level of understanding before explaining a new idea
- Intuitively weighing the many factors affecting success of development and marketing tasks
- Perceptively adopting a style of speech that suits a particular listener
- Negotiating fair compromises among disagreeing professionals
- Patiently empathizing with the obstacles and frustrations workers at all levels encounter in trying to do their jobs
- Logically analyzing and investigating behavioral problems to find their underlying causes
- Creatively developing unique ways of approaching and solving technical problems
- Great at encouraging team effort on river rafting trips

Read this list of skills and quickly assign each to a group. You will have to make some assumptions in this case, since you don't have David's experience or intuition. Remember, you may assign the same skill to more than one group. Give each group a temporary name that desribe the skills it contains. When you're finished, read on and see how David clustered his own skills.

David's Clusters

Researching, Analyzing, and Presenting
- Confidently presenting ideas before large audiences
- Effectively questioning people I don't know while I'm traveling

- Persistently perfecting speeches
- Naturally maintaining a sense of humor when challenged
- Successfully persuading others to accept another point of view
- Working on every detail of a presentation plan with great care
- Perceptively adopting a style of speech that suits a particular listener

Dedicated Problem-Solving Team Member

- Enthusiastically participating in a highly committed team
- Objectively weighing the pros and cons of work alternatives
- Intuitively weighing the many factors affecting success of development and marketing tasks
- Creatively developing unique ways of approaching and solving technical problems

Effectively Managing Personnel

- Tactfully calming down excited people
- Patiently helping others to learn a new skill
- Naturally maintaining a sense of humor when challenged
- Negotiating fair compromises among disagreeing professionals
- Patiently empathizing with the obstacles and frustrations workers at all levels encounter in trying to do their jobs
- Logically analyzing and investigating behavioral problems to find their underlying causes
- Great at encouraging team effort on river rafting trips

Teaching

- Confidently presenting ideas before large audiences
- Patiently helping others to learn a new skill
- Naturally maintaining a sense of humor when challenged
- Accurately assessing an audience's level of understanding before explaining a new idea
- Perceptively adopting a style of speech that suits a particular listener

Compare David's clusters with the ones you came up with using his skills list. Chances are they are different. It might seem logical to you to put "successfully persuading others . . ." into a teaching category. But David intuitively knew that wasn't right for him, because "persuading" wasn't part of his teaching style. You can see why it's important for each person to trust his or her own instincts and select clusters alone, without advice from others.

This was just a practice to give you a sense of how to cluster. Now, as you go to your own skill cards, you will have many more skills to peruse and will end up with more clusters.

Refining Your Skill Clusters

After your first pass at forming skill clusters, put them aside for at least 24 hours and then come back to them for review. Line up your clusters. Fan out each group so you can read the cards. Do you still feel comfortable with the way the cards are grouped? If some cards seem vague, check the code on the back and look at the life story they came from. Flesh out the description on the cards until they make an understandable statement. You may want to move some cards or make more duplicates. If you can't decide where a card belongs, follow your first instinct.

You probably have between 8 and 18 clusters. More than 18 are too many to remember easily; fewer than 8 won't do justice to your talents. If you are outside these boundaries, check the clues below.

When you have completed your review, you are ready to give your clusters permanent names.

NEED CLUES?

- If you have too few clusters you may need to write more life stories or cull more skills from the stories you have.
- Make sure you have written about all the significant events in your life and add different types of activities.

- You may need some fresh insights. Ask some new people to join you in practicing skill identification.
- If you have too many clusters you probably have several similar groups. Pick up any vague clusters and reassign the skill cards.

S. GROSS

Naming Clusters

Now is a good time to ask friends to join the game. The people with whom you did skill identification might help, especially if they are working through the same process. You can also choose someone outside that group; if you do, ask the smartest, most insightful, most articulate person you know. If you don't have a helper, go ahead on your own. You can always get advice later if you feel you need it. Alone or with a friend, this is the way to name clusters.

1. Select one cluster and spread all of the cards out in front of you with the temporary name card at the top.

2. With a highlighter (or on a separate sheet of paper) pick out the key words on each skill card.

3. On a separate sheet of paper jot down any words or phrases implied but not actually written on the cards.

4. Imagine you will have 10 seconds to describe this functional ability. What would you call it? Construct a name from your key words. Try using the same format you used when you named skills: "How Well," "What," and "Where."

The names you have given your clusters represent your super skills. A super skills signifies an area in which you have a high level of interest and competence. Super skills derive directly from the experiences you have captured in your clusters. They are the skills that have consistently proved to be rewarding, in terms of both results and personal satisfaction.

In later chapters, you will use super skills to describe how your strongest capabilities can meet the needs of potential employer. But for now, read on to learn how David went about selecting his super skills from his clusters.

David's Cluster Names

David went through one of his clusters, the one temporarily named Researching, Analyzing, and Presenting, and highlighted on each skill card the key words that seemed to define the essence of the cluster. His highlighted skill cards looked like this:

- *Confidently presenting* ideas before large audiences
- Effectively *questioning* people I don't know while I'm traveling
- *Persistently* working on speech formats and technical tasks
- Naturally maintaining a sense of *humor* when challenged
- Successfully *persuading* others to accept another point of view
- Working on every detail of a presentation plan with great care
- *Perceptively* adopting a style of speech that suits a particular listener

He also made notes about other skills he knew were related to the cluster, even though they did not appear on a card.

Key words highlighted:	Not highlighted, but known:
• confidently	
• presenting	• researching
• questioning	• one-on-one
• persistently	• adapting
• humor	• small groups
• persuading	• concepts
• perceptively	

Considering these two lists, David named his cluster, By Means of Careful Research and Preparation, Making Convincing Presentations with Humor to Many Types of Audiences. This "super skill" card captures the essence of all the cards gathered in that one cluster.

Let's look at another of David's clusters, the one temporarily named, Dedicated Problem-Solving Team Member. Here are his highlighted skill cards:

■ Enthusiastically participating in a highly *committed team*

■ *Objectively* weighing the pros and cons of work alternatives

■ *Intuitively* weighing the many factors affecting accomplishment of *academic, marketing, and development* tasks

■ *Creatively* developing unique ways of approaching and solving technical problems

Key words highlighted:	Not highlighted, but known:
• team	• dedicated
• committed	• monitoring
• objectively	• performing
• intuitively	
• academic, marketing, development	
• creatively	

David's final name for his cluster: Functioning With Almost Intuitive Creativity on Development and Marketing Tasks When Part of a Committed Team.

NEED CLUES?

- When a card doesn't seem to fit anywhere, check the reference code on the back. Referring to the life story will help you place it comfortably.
- Thinking too hard about which card goes where interferes with your intuition (which is almost always accurate).

- Sometimes several clusters form at the same time; conversely, sometimes you may see several cards at once which all belong in one cluster.
- The number of cards in a cluster often varies dramatically. Size is not necessarily an indication of value.

To Sum Up

Naming your skill clusters is the synthesis of all the time and effort you have spent in self-discovery. This is a major achievement. Knowing your super skills builds the foundation for all your future endeavors and gives you a deci-sive, winning edge in every goal you go after. When you understand how to communicate your skills accurately, succinctly, and with total conviction, you will hand decision-makers the information they need to decide on you.

Nothing sells as well as the truth.

Knowing your super skills is one thing; convincingly talking about them to others is another. Two important activities will help you present your super skills. When you are ready, continue on.

CHAPTER FIVE

Talking About Yourself

YOU HAVE COMPLETED the most important part of the Crystal-Barkley process: You are clear about your abilities and qualities, which in large measure describe who you are. Two activities in this chapter will help you make this information invaluable in your job search, especially if you are looking for a position in a field different from your present work. You will learn to effectively articulate your super skills, a skill in itself and one which will help potential employers know you're the right person for the job. You'll also decide which of these skills you most want to use on the job. *You have the ability—and the right—to decide which of your super skills you will use most often in your future work.* This is one important way to ensure that you will feel satisfied and be productive on the job.

COMING UP

A newly articulate you, able to confidently describe your strongest skills.

☞ Become polished in describing each skill cluster in terms of when you did it; where you did it; the results you got by doing it.

☞ Create a priority among skill clusters according to how much you enjoy using the skills, and how good you are at doing them.

☞ Determine your five top super skills—those you're both good at and enjoy.

35

Conveying Your Talents

Let's look at an exchange that took place between Elizabeth and a prospective employer when she was seeking interim work as a salesperson during the busy holiday season. Elizabeth was taking a needed break from writing while she tried to determine what she really wanted to be doing with her life.

Employer: Can you tell me why I should hire you rather than one of the other candidates?

Elizabeth: Here are a couple of good reasons. I have a track record for troubleshooting very effectively with customers, and I can also work well under pressure.

Employer: That sounds great, but I wonder if you've experienced anything as hectic as what we face here each day?

At this point Elizabeth knew that she must deliver proof that she was up to the demands of the job. Having prepared well, she did not hesitate at all.

Elizabeth: Ever since my first real job—as an art camp counselor, where the campers' rallying cry was 'Get the counselor!'—I've been good at coping with pressure. Even then I could instill discipline without interfering with self-expression and creativity. Within two weeks, my campers were playing organized games, making crafts, and could even be left alone for periods of time.

A more recent example of my skill at handling pressure was my work as a customer-service supervisor at a busy mail-order house. The company frequently was slow sending out merchandise. I often had to intervene to handle irate customers. I always responded politely to their angry comments and assured them I would personally investigate and get back to them. As a result, the company's cancellation frequency was reduced by 50 percent. In fact, I received a promotion.

Without hesitation, Elizabeth convincingly delivered evidence that backed up her claims. She would have had a hard time doing so if she hadn't been well prepared. Her preparation involved constructing "talking papers."

A talking paper is a brief summary of the specific occasions when you used a particular super skill and the results you achieved. You need to prepare a talking paper for each of your super skills (clusters).

Creating Talking Papers

Label the next tab in your notebook or computer *Talking Papers*. At the top of a fresh page, write the name of one of your skill clusters. Let's say one of your clusters is "Excellent at moderating differing viewpoints in public presentations." Divide the page into three columns, headed "Where," "When," "With What Results."

In the first column write one place where you remember using this super skill. Suppose it was "at the cable-television roundtable concerning free speech on college campuses."

"I don't like being tested!"

In the middle column write when (the actual dates or time period) you did this, e.g., "February 1992."

In the third column, list *all* the results you can remember. Be specific. If possible, include numbers and quantities or any other objective evidence. Comments from other people and published reviews will also work as evidence.

- More than 300 call-ins—a record.

- Program rebroadcast six times.

- Panelists said 'First time we've talked together without losing our tempers.'

Consider the first entry on Elizabeth's talking paper, which she used as an example to convince her potential interim employer.

NAME OF SUPER SKILL: Diplomatically Handling Retail Customers or Clients in High Pressure Situations

WHERE	WHEN	WITH WHAT RESULTS
L. Franklin mail-order house, Freeport, NY	1986–88	Customers calmed down. Cancellation frequency reduced by 50%. Was promoted to supervisor after six months.

Notice that Elizabeth is being specific and that one result tends to lead to another. Because she calmed down customers she had time to investigate their complaints and realistically reassure them; as a result, the cancellation frequency was reduced, leading to her promotion. Elizabeth then went on to list other incidences when this same super skill was used.

Now, do your own. You might want to start by looking through David's talking paper on the facing page. Then begin listing specific occasions when you used the super skill you identified and write down all the proof you can muster. When you have exhausted your memory, go to another super skill (start a new page or computer heading for each one). Continue until you have created a talking paper for each of your super skills.

NEED CLUES?

- Can't remember anything that happened? Check some of the codes on the backs of the skill cards in that cluster. Go to the very spot in your life stories where you demonstrated a particular skill.

- Can't find any hard evidence? Try to recall what happened on this particular occasion. What did people say to you? Was there an upturn in sales, orders, revenue, telephone response? A reduction in waiting time? Fewer returns? If so, by how much? If you can, *use numbers.*

- Be specific about feedback from others. "After my speech, *eight* people said they were going to look into changing their accounting systems because of my remarks."

- Think of secondary results: "Five of them were so happy with the changed system that they later became regular customers of the company and bought other software products."

- Writing cryptic notes to yourself is okay; you're creating reminders to yourself, not prose for publication.

- It's also okay to refer to events from your youth; in fact, youthful experiences can be very convincing—remember Elizabeth's stint as a camp counselor.

- Personal gain also illustrates positive results: "I ended up getting three more speaking engagements."

- Your events and results do not need to be chronological.

David's Talking Paper

SUPER SKILL: By Means of Careful Research and Preparation Making Convincing Presentations With Humor to Many Types of Audiences

WHERE	WHEN	WITH WHAT RESULTS
High school	1960s	On debating team, which was a big deal, like being on a sports team. Over 4 years, won 17 awards.
High school	Senior year	Chosen "Debater of the Year."
Albuquerque	1966	Represented region at national tournament; came in sixth.
Yale	1966	Won one debate and one extemporaneous speaking contest in university-wide tournament.

Chicago area	1970s	Was selected at least a dozen times to speak on behalf of charities at service clubs.
Yale	1970s	Largely due to speaking abilities, elected sophomore class vice president, junior class president, and ran for student body president.
Darden School, University of Virginia	1980	Held my own comfortably in classroom debate. Named team chair of negotiation role play—our team won.
First Interstate	1980s	Favorable reaction to my board-level presentations called attention to me—resulted in CEO naming me to special SWAT team.
Los Angeles	1994–95	Regular speaker for Goodwill Industries, resulting in more than $30K in increased support. Led to being asked to promote Habitat for Humanity.

Your Personal Best

Once you have created a talking paper for each super skill, you are ready for one final task of self discovery (for now!).

Put away your clusters of skill cards. From now on, your talking papers, which ultimately you will commit to memory, represent your skills. This is a far more manageable way to present yourself than carrying around stacks of skill cards.

Your final job is to decide which super skills you want to use most in your work. You have two criteria to help you: enjoyment and competence. You may have worried that despite your ability, you don't really enjoy some of your super skills. Now is your chance to put them toward the bottom of your list.

■ Spread out your talking papers on a broad surface where you can see them all at once. Ask yourself, "Which one do I absolutely most enjoy using?" Take the paper you chose and put it aside.

■ From among those left, which do you enjoy next best? Select the second talking paper and put it under the first one.

■ *Do not mark the talking papers.*

■ Continue the selection process until all of your talking papers are in order.

■ Review them. In the *Talking Papers* section of your notebook or computer, start a new heading: "Talking Papers in Order of Enjoyment." Write down in the order you just selected the names of each talking paper. Put your talking papers away until another day.

■ On a new day, without looking at your previous work, spread out your talking papers again. Ask yourself, "Which of these do I *know* I perform the best?" Place your choice to one side.

■ Ask yourself, "Which super skill do I perform the next best?" Put that talking paper under your first choice. Continue the selection process until all of your talking papers are in order, according to your competence.

■ Review them. In your notebook or computer, start a new heading: "Talking Papers in Order of Competence." Make a new list of the names of the talking papers.

You are now ready to blend the two lists into one final list that will put your super skills in priority order. Place your two lists side by side. The two lists are never identical; they usually look something like this (imagine the numbers stand for the names of your talking papers):

Enjoyment List	Competence List
1	5
2	3
3	1
4	8
5	10
6	7
7	2
8	4
9	6
10	9

If you draw lines between the matching talking papers, you will get their final position. If a talking paper is at position 1 in one column and position 3 in the other, it will end up at position 2, which in the drawing below is first place. See how it's done.

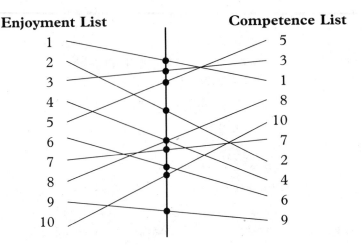

Enjoyment List   **Competence List**

While number 1 on enjoyment still comes up first on the blended list, notice that 2 comes up fourth, 3 is second, and 4 is fifth, in the same position as 8. Number 7 stays in seventh, 6 is eighth, just ahead of 10, and number 9 is now tenth.

When there is a tie (as in the case of 4 and 8 in the illustration), resolve it in favor of the enjoyment side; most of us do better at the things we like doing.

To Sum Up

With your talking papers in their preferred order, you have almost completed the *Who Am I?* section of this book. As you get ready to move into the next section, you will begin to feel the full impact of this work. Your top five super skills will become a prominent part of your final decisions concerning work. In fact, it's likely that anyone observing you perform one of these super skills will be impressed at how naturally it comes to you.

You will use a skill set at the bottom of your list only if the work also uses your top talents. You would never choose work that centers around one of your lower-level skill groups.

Putting your super skills in order also helps you make good decisions about future education and training. If a super skill is high on your enjoyment list but low on your competence list, you might want to seek work that offers good on-the-job training for this particular skill, find an employer who will sponsor outside training, go back to school, or take a special course to get the training yourself. Because schooling is a substantial investment of time and money, thoroughly research your field of interest before deciding whether this is the best route. There are many ways to learn: Never choose school simply because you believe the credentials will get you the job. A lot of sad people are wandering in and out of personnel offices today who thought the right degree would solve their work problem. Today's working world requires more than credentials, and sometimes the credentials you believed were essential aren't as important as you thought.

> *Iffen you dunnit,*
> *it ain't braggin.*
> —South Carolina country man

You initially formed your skill clusters without regard to time or place. This gave you the opportunity to see how childhood skills might be used in the service of sophisticated endeavors. Some of your true talents and all of your personality skills were evident in early childhood, and including them in your skill clusters may be the first time you have taken advantage of their power. Later, when you developed talking papers, you attached your skill clusters to specific events, thereby equipping yourself to effectively present your top skills to a potential employer and back them up with hard evidence.

You are fully loaded and almost ready to go. But before you start out, there's one more critical piece to fit into your personal puzzle.

Uncovering Values

I F YOU COULD design a perfect work situation for yourself, what element in it would be most important? Yes, of course, the people. The right co-workers can make or break a job. Your work environment also has a direct impact on job satisfaction. Poor working conditions can make you unhappy on the job, even if you enjoy your responsibilities. Finally, the community you live in affects your overall satisfaction. Too many of us put considerations about where we live second to getting a good job. But if you aren't thriving in your community, it's hard to thrive at work. Fortunately, these factors are within your control. Thousands of our clients have come up with requirements for their work and living environments and then gone out and either found or created work that met them. You can too.

COMING UP

A way to help ensure that you work among people you like in a pleasant environment and live in a community you love.

☞ Pinpoint the qualities that are most important to you in people, community, and workplace.

☞ Determine those qualities you prize most.

☞ Figure out the characteristics you dislike (and those you dislike most) with regard to people, community, and workplace.

☞ Gain a clear picture of your ideal surroundings.

Surrounding Yourself With the Right People

How many times have you liked a particular job but disliked your co-workers? Perhaps your personalities clashed or they didn't have your standards; or perhaps your boss was overbearing. Such problems happen all the time, because most people don't realize that part of choosing the right job is choosing the people you work with.

Even in jobs that don't require much personal day-to-day contact with people, your interactions with people affect you. You might see your boss only occasionally, but if you don't get along, he or she will not give you a good appraisal or might not pass interesting projects along to you. You may work side-by-side with only one person, but if that colleague's personality or work habits grate on you, you will find life at work difficult.

It takes foresight to avoid the trap of walking into an on-the-job snakepit, but it is possible to surround yourself with people who support your work and make you feel good. The first step is to figure out what you want and need in your co-workers.

Up to a point, most of us share similar likes and dislikes with regard to people. We value qualities such as honesty, generosity, and friendliness, and dislike such qualities as dishonesty, rudeness, and conceit. However, there are many other qualities about which we would disagree. You might like the traits of competitiveness, assertiveness, and outspokenness, whereas someone else might find them too strong, preferring colleagues who are easygoing and free-spirited.

Starting a "Likes" List

Label the next tab in your notebook or computer: *My Values*. At the top of a fresh sheet of paper write "People Values." Draw a line down the middle; head the left-hand column "Likes" and the right-hand column "Dislikes."

Write down all the "likes" you can think of. Describe your likes in adjectives (friendly, loyal), nouns (team player), or phrases (willing to take risks). Short reminders, rather than essays, are what you want here.

You can increase your list of likes by recalling the many people you know and have dealt with at different times of your life: friends, family,

NEED CLUES?

- Think about people who are fun. Picture each person clearly and ask yourself, "Why do I like being with this person?"
- Do you recall someone you liked immediately on meeting? What did you find so appealing about that person?
- Reflect on your past. Who were your favorite people? A grade school teacher? A camp counselor? A classmate?

- Perhaps you have read about someone you admire. What qualities did this person have that appealed to you?
- Sometimes we neglect to list the obvious. For example, "I like people who like me."
- Taking one clue at a time, write down all the likes you discover; go through all five of the above clues.

teachers, co-workers, your spouse. Remember one person at a time and write down the traits you like about each.

You probably have even more "likes" than you've listed. To further spur your thinking, take a look at the more than 100 examples in the box on the next page. For each ask yourself, "Is this quality important to me?" If so, add it—or another word that it suggests—to your list.

Starting a "Dislikes" List

When you have exhausted your "likes," take a look at the other side of the people question. Is there anything you just can't stand in a person? Think of someone you have tried to avoid or couldn't wait to get away from. What was it about him or her? Here's your chance to list all the things about people that you dislike. In the right-hand column of your paper, list all the "dislikes" you can think of.

Don't worry about being too picky. It's true that nobody is perfect and we all have our faults. But there are certain traits each of us particularly dislikes, and there's no reason to choose a work environment where those traits are likely to flourish. You will have an opportunity to refine your list. For now, let 'er rip!

When you run out of ideas, take a look at the box on page 49 listing "dislikes" other people have mentioned. You'll notice that some of the "dislikes" also appeared on the "likes" list. That's simply because what one person values, another may abhor. For example, some people like eccentricity; others can't stand it.

POSSIBLE "LIKES"

- Adventurous
- Ambitious
- Analytical
- Appreciative
- Artistic
- Assertive
- Attractive
- Brave
- Calm
- Caring
- Carry their share
- Charming
- Clever
- Committed
- Communicative
- Compassionate
- Competent
- Competitive
- Conservative
- Conversational
- Cooperative
- Courageous
- Creative
- Decisive
- Dependable
- Determined
- Direct
- Discriminating
- Dutiful
- Easygoing
- Eccentric
- Efficient
- Emotional
- Empathetic
- Energetic
- Enterprising
- Enthusiastic
- Ethical
- Exciting

- Fair
- Flexible
- Forgiving
- Frank
- Free-spirited
- Friendly
- Generous
- Gentle
- Giving
- Good listener
- Gregarious
- Happy
- Hardworking
- Honest
- Humane
- Humble
- Idealistic
- Independent
- Individualistic
- Informal
- Innocent
- Inquisitive
- Intellectual
- Intelligent
- Intense
- Kind
- Knowledgeable
- Liberal
- Loving
- Loyal
- Motivated
- Musical
- Neat
- Objective
- Open-minded
- Optimistic
- Original
- Outspoken
- Patient

- Perceptive
- Personable
- Playful
- Polite
- Popular
- Practical
- Principled
- Progressive
- Prompt
- Realistic
- Reflective
- Reliable
- Resourceful
- Responsible
- Self-possessed
- Self-disciplined
- Self-improving
- Sense of humor
- Sensitive
- Serene
- Silly
- Sincere
- Sociable
- Socially responsible
- Sophisticated
- Spiritual
- Stimulating
- Surprising
- Talented
- Thoughtful
- Tolerant
- Traditional
- Trusting
- Unpredictable
- Warm
- Well-rounded
- Witty
- Worldly

POSSIBLE "DISLIKES"

- Aggressive
- Ambitious
- Analytical
- Angry
- Antisocial
- Apathetic
- Arrogant
- Backstabbing
- Bigoted
- Blamer
- Boring
- Brusque
- Cheater
- Close-minded
- Cold
- Complacent
- Complainer
- Compulsive
- Conceited
- Condescending
- Cowardly
- Critical
- Crude
- Cruel
- Cynical
- Deceitful
- Defensive
- Demanding
- Dependent
- Devious
- Dishonest
- Disloyal
- Disrespectful
- Doesn't listen
- Dogmatic
- Eccentric
- Egotistical
- Emotional
- Envious

- Fanatic
- Fake
- Formal
- Gossipy
- Gregarious
- Gullible
- Hostile
- Hypocritical
- Ignorant
- Immature
- Impatient
- Impersonal
- Incompetent
- Inconsiderate
- Inhibited
- Insensitive
- Intellectual
- Intimidating
- Intolerant
- Irresponsible
- Jealous
- Know-it-all
- Lazy
- Loud
- Manipulative
- Materialistic
- Mean
- Messy
- Money-grubbing
- Moody
- Nitpicking
- Nosy
- Obsequious
- Obstinate
- Opinionated
- Overbearing
- Passive
- Perfectionist
- Pessimistic

- Petty
- Prejudiced
- Pretentious
- Procrastinating
- Resentful
- Sarcastic
- Self-righteous
- Sexist
- Showy
- Silly
- Simplistic
- Sleazy
- Sloppy
- Slow
- Smoker
- Snobby
- Stingy
- Stubborn
- Stuck-up
- Stupid
- Superficial
- Suspicious
- Taciturn
- Tactless
- Talkative
- Tasteless
- Thoughtless
- Traditional
- Two-faced
- Uncooperative
- Undependable
- Unethical
- Unfriendly
- Untruthful
- Vulgar
- Weird
- Whiny
- Work-shirking
- Zealot

S. GROSS

NEED CLUES?

- Think about the people you deliberately avoid. What bothers you most about them?
- What kind of habits really turn you off? It could be the way someone talks, behaves, or even takes care of his or her workplace.
- Think of fictional characters—which ones seemed vile? Why were they so unlikable?
- Who's in the news? Is there someone you think is awful? What did this person do or say that belongs on your list?

- Review your list of likes. Are opposites suggested? (Honest/Dishonest; Neat/Messy.) Not every "like" will have an opposite "dislike." For example, you may prefer someone who is creative but not actually dislike a person who lacks creativity.
- Think of people you've met at different times of your life. Do you remember any teachers you disliked? Any bosses who upset you? Any relationships that ended because of something you didn't like about the individual?

Refining Your Lists

Once your lists are very long, you're ready to decide which traits are most important to you. Read down your "likes" list and put an asterisk next to any quality you absolutely need in the people with whom you work. Do you really *need* people around you with a "sense of humor," who are "smart," or who "respect" you? This is your chance to clarify your priorities about people. You may prefer that co-workers have the qualities you skip over, but these qualities or traits are not essential to you.

Too Few or Too Many Likes?

If you have starred only one or two items on your "likes" list, you may be someone who indiscriminately accepts people. You like almost everyone, as long as he or she is honest and hard-working. You may have trained yourself to see the good side of people or to accept them for what they are. This is certainly a good habit, but you should still try to express your true feelings about what you need in people. Take another look.

By contrast, if you have starred dozens of items on your "likes" list, you may be very particular about people, or you may have starred qualities that are not really essential. Take another look at the items you selected. Must they all remain on the "need" list?

Repeat the same selection process with your "dislikes" list. Put an asterisk next to any quality you absolutely reject in people. For example, do you find it intolerable to be around people who are bigoted, self-centered, or impatient?

Why You're Doing This

Why is it so important to identify your likes and dislikes about people? Granted, it's unrealistic to expect to find a working environment where everybody has all of the qualities you like and none of the qualities you dislike. But you can focus on the traits that matter the most to you.

Suppose you have placed "greedy" on your "reject" list. Sometime later, suppose you are considering a job selling a product that interests you and allows you to use some of your best skills. So far, so good.

When you meet your potential coworkers, however, you learn that most of them will do anything to get the sale, up to and including being deceitful. They refer to customers as "marks" and talk constantly about being how much money they're making. They seem oblivious to the product itself or to the needs and concerns of those who buy from them. You decide to decline this opportunity because you know that you absolutely cannot tolerate greed in people you spend time with.

Working Conditions

In addition to the people you work with, it's important that you're satisfied with your working conditions. Everybody has a vision of a terrific working situation. Give yourself a few minutes to analyze exactly what elements are involved for you. Their presence or absence can make the difference between misery and satisfaction.

Julia, one of our clients, recalled the first day she walked into a new job in a large insurance corporation. "I had seen the set-up briefly during my interview, but I didn't think much about it. But when I came in the first day, I felt uneasy. I was put off by the huge open office space—long rows of desks blanketing the entire floor, with executive offices around the perimeter, and a row of windowless prefab inside offices

"Whoever planned this job never took into consideration 'leg cramps.'"

down the middle. I had one of the little inside offices. The first day, the office manager came around and handed me my lunch and coffee break schedule, telling me to conform to the schedule no matter what I was doing. This was some time ago and I was the only woman "junior executive." I was expected to adhere to the secretaries' schedule, even though I didn't have to cover anyone's phone. I immediately bristled and from then on, for two whole years, I resisted every rule and regulation of the company. In all that time, it never occurred to me that

> *Your negotiating leverage is greatest when going into a job, so be sure of what you want.*

I could have looked for a job that offered a working environment I'd have enjoyed. I had expected to take the best job I was offered, but besides money, I had never thought about what elements make a job 'best.'"

Another "Likes" and "Dislikes" List

Your next heading is "Working Conditions." As you have done before, on the left note everything important to you in a working environment—the number of people, the physical layout, and how you are managed. Try to imagine what your ideal workplace is like:

■ How many people are around you?

■ Is it a bustling or quiet environment?

■ Are you at a desk, in a factory, traveling, at customer sites, outdoors, or elsewhere?

■ Do you have your own office? If so, what does it look like?

■ How are people dressed?

■ Is it a small, medium, or large organization?

■ Do you follow a clear set of guidelines and procedures on the job, or do you work things out on your own?

■ Are you self-employed or working for someone else?

■ If you are working for someone, how are you treated?

■ What are your hours? Nine to five? An evening shift?

Think about all of these issues. Then close your eyes and picture your ideal workplace. Study the details in your mind's eye before returning to pen and paper to record more items.

NEED CLUES?

- Think of the jobs you've had in the past, including any part-time work. Recall each one and ask yourself, "What particular aspects of the working conditions appealed to me?"
- Think back on your experiences in school, church, and clubs.

What did you like most about these situations?
- Think about books, television shows, and movies in which people are portrayed in their working environments. Do you remember any that particularly appealed to you?

Elizabeth had no difficulty starting her list:

■ Immediate access to supervisor who can "yes" or "no" ideas

■ Clean, well-lit, quiet room to work in

■ Window

■ Good ventilation, good temperature control

■ Open channels of communications with superiors

■ Speed—boss and co-workers like getting to solutions fast

■ Camaraderie among co-workers

■ Intelligent, competent co-workers—people who enjoy their work are good at it

■ Regularly given new responsibilities

■ Supportive environment where people show their appreciation for what you do, both in terms of financial bonuses and actually saying "You did a good job." (This is particularly important for us writers and artists, who absolutely must have feedback or we'll go home wanting to kill ourselves. There's just no other way to gauge success.)

■ Casual dress—a place where a person's work speaks more loudly than appearance

■ Flexible hours that depend on deadlines and job requirements rather than preset schedules or company rules

■ A sense of the business as a whole and my role within the large scheme of things (not just my narrow function)

When you have exhausted your descriptions of likes, turn to your dislikes. Think of all the things you hated on a job or could have done without. Take a look at the Need Clues? box on the previous page and turn the questions around to reveal working conditions that you dislike. Also take a look at the box on the next page. It contains a list of dislikes that other people have mentioned about their working conditions. You may find it useful to ask yourself, "Would I mind if this situation were part of my job?" If an item would bother you, add it to your list. Once you're sure you've covered all the bases, select your "need" and "reject" items as before.

Community Considerations

Obviously, where you live is integral to your happiness. But many job seekers today give community environment a low priority because they believe they have to "go where the jobs are." They believe that making a list of requirements about a place to live restricts their career opportunities. Not so. Identifying your community preferences can actually help, not hinder, your career.

People always perform better when their surroundings offer them activities that refresh and stimulate them. You save time and reduce frustration by starting a job search or seeking relocation in geographic areas of choice. If you think only about "the job," you may accidentally wind up somewhere you really hate or somewhere that doesn't offer the activities and institutions you most enjoy. One music-loving client of ours took a fabulously high-paying job in a midwestern city, only to find that she was miserable because the area had little in the way of cultural activity and the people she met weren't interested in creating cultural events. If you take the time to analyze what's important to you in the way of community values, you'll have the opportunity to look before you leap.

At the top of a fresh sheet of paper write: "Community Values". Draw a line down the middle; head the left-hand column "Likes" and the right-hand column "Dislikes." In exactly the same way as you did for people characteristics, write down all the community "likes" you can think of. Picture the many different places you have lived, vacationed, or visited—one place at a time, remember what you liked about each.

UNPLEASANT WORKING CONDITIONS

- Unattractive building (run-down, institutional, sterile)
- Cramped work space
- Controlled environment (sealed windows, fluorescent lights)
- Dirty or sloppy working conditions
- Environmentally polluted (lack of good ventilation, fumes, smoking, dust, unpleasant odors)
- Unappealing location (long commute, bad neighborhood, few services nearby)
- No privacy
- Noisy
- No windows
- Lack of recognition for a job well done
- Pressure or stress artificially induced to keep employees revved up and off balance
- Distrustful management
- Harsh criticism
- Too tight or too frequent deadlines
- One-way communications only
- Emphasis on quantity at the expense of quality
- Decisions made exclusively by higher-ups
- Departments or work groups fighting each other
- Unrealistic goals or expectations
- Hard to see or measure results of job performance
- Promotions not based on ability
- Size of raises not based on performance
- Static industry
- Unstable industry or organization
- Excessive paperwork
- Inadequate training
- Repetitious or routine work
- Lack of teamwork
- Job not challenging
- No opportunity to be creative
- Constantly interrupted
- Isolated from co-workers
- Long hours
- Restrictive dress code
- Expected to socialize with co-workers and clients after hours
- Too much traveling
- Lots of office gossip
- Working the late shift
- Expected to work late and on weekends
- Underpaid
- Work does not make a tangible contribution to society

For now, forget about whether a perfect place exists. Simply make your list, thinking about:

- Your geographic preference (the Southwest; Italy; the West Coast)
- Weather (hot, cool, dry, humid, a four-season climate)
- Size of the community and kinds of people who live there
- Appearance of the landscape

- Nearby natural resources (ocean, mountains, farmland)
- Look of the community (modern homes, historic districts)
- Entertainment and leisure facilities available (theater, nightclubs, golf courses)
- Economic and professional base (high-tech, pharmaceutical, financial, publishing, academic)

As you expand your own list, you might get some ideas from the items on David's list, below, which turned out to be fairly short, even before pared down to his "needs."

- Size of the community and kinds of people who live there
- Mild weather (not too hot, not too cold)
- Mountains nearby, with snow in wintertime
- High frequency of clear skies
- Large, clean city with effective public-transportation system
- Cultural diversity
- Access to a major, first-rate university
- Low crime
- Dynamic economy

When you have exhausted your descriptions of likes, make your "dislikes" list. These items will relate to many of the same issues: size, location, appearance, climate, and so on. Here is David's "dislikes" list—the rejects—which in some ways is a reverse template of his previous list.

■ Extremes in climate

■ Cultural narrowness

■ Close juxtaposition of very rich and very poor

■ High crime rate

■ Dirty sidewalks, streets, and old, dirty buildings

■ Lack of a first-rate university

■ Lack of mass transit

Again, Refining Your Lists

Do you really need "ocean views," "lots of movie theaters," or "warm weather year-round"? This is your chance to clarify your priorities about community. Be selective about which items you absolutely need. Rarely would even the best location have every quality you like. Asterisk only those items you find essential.

NEED CLUES?

Try completing these phrases. I don't want to live in a community that:

• Is at or near these geographic locations: _____.

• Has _____ weather.

• Doesn't have a good selection of _____.

• Is bigger (or smaller) than _____ _____.

• Doesn't have leisure facilities for _____.

• Has too many (or too few) people who are _____.

• Is lacking in _____ scenery.

• Is not near natural resources of _____.

• Has too many (or too few) houses (or apartments) that are _____.

• Has too many (or too few) ____ ____ businesses or organizations.

• Can you recall a time when you immediately disliked a place? Why?

• Think about places you *never* wanted to visit. Exactly what makes each of these places seem unappealing?

Go ahead, expand your list.

Now, do the same for the reverse side. Would you really find it intolerable to live in a community that has "heavy traffic," "no mountains nearby," or a "large population"?

If you have only a few dislikes, you may be someone who would find a wide variety of communities acceptable. One person said she could live almost anywhere as long as the crime rate and air pollution were not excessive. Other people are much more particular about their community environment. If your list of dislikes is very, very long, rethink it and try prioritizing the items.

Making choices about the kind of community where you want to live can make an enormous difference to your future work happiness. Expressing your true feelings about what you can and cannot accept in communities puts you in a much better position to make good decisions about your future.

To Sum Up

Take a look at the starred items on your "likes" and "dislikes" lists. Here, you have outlined your ideal (and not-so-ideal) conditions related to people, workplace, and community.

As you move toward choosing the right work for you in Parts Two and Three, the items on these lists will help shape your list of "criteria" that will ultimately determine your first, second, and third choices among potential employers.

Part Two

WHERE AM I GOING?

*Uncovering your
interests and goals*

CHAPTER SEVEN

What Do You Want Out Of Life?

HAVING A CLEAR sense of your skills and values is an advantage that not many people have—one that should give you tremendous self-confidence. But there's another step; you've got to figure out how you want to apply your talents and to what end. Doing so will give you a focus and confidence that will be very attractive to potential employers. At Crystal-Barkley, we refer to this as finding your central mission or your goals. It's a matter of getting in touch with the inner truth about you.

It's a revelation for some people to discover that they have an inner calling; some even hesitate to explore for fear that when they look inside nothing will be there. We can assure you that within everyone lies a personal mission, and that if you complete the activities in this and the following three chapters you'll

COMING UP

A sense that you can live and work in a way that's in tune with what you're all about.

☞ Recapture your dreams—some of which may date back to your very early years—and discover how these might be made practical in today's world.

☞ Complete a systematic, yet deceptively playful set of activities and begin to uncover your personal goals.

☞ Talk to people who knew you well as a child and may remember what you dreamed of doing with your life.

find yours, and have an adventure doing it. Once you do, you will feel exhilarated and your discovery will illuminate the rest of your life.

"Oh, no," you might say, "I'm not that complex!" Don't you believe it. One of our happy rewards at Crystal-Barkley has been discovering layers of richness in people's lives. No one's life is simple, as you'll discover once you know how to look for the goals that give you your drive.

What David Remembered

When David came to Crystal-Barkley, he knew he was seeking a new direction for himself, although he was not prepared to go about it in the fun-loving way we proposed. He expected the Crystal-Barkley process to be like work. Of course, it *was* work to assemble enough life stories; when it came to discovering his goals, however, it seemed like a vacation.

We asked David if he could recall what he used to dream about doing as a child. What would he answer when adults asked him what he wanted to be when he grew up?

David immediately responded, "I always felt very uncomfortable when grown-ups asked me that question because I knew I didn't want to be a stockbroker like my father. But I didn't know anything else to *be* that would be acceptable."

David said he usually answered something like "Oh, I dunno, maybe an architect," a career in which he had no interest at all. He knew there were teachers and camp counselors and people who worked

> *It's not enough to know who you are. You must eventually answer the question "What am I for?"*

in stores, but these occupations didn't seem like serious work—and he knew work was serious.

"I loved being part of a comfortable, conservative family, but my ideas were different from the ones I heard my parents discussing around the dinner table," he explained.

As David thought back, he remembered more. "I built a treehouse in the wooded area behind our backyard," he said. "I used to imagine this was a camouflaged lookout on a ranch I lived on out West. Mountains surrounded the ranch and a river ran through the property. A large cabin was perched on a bluff overlooking the river and the barn was behind it, around a bend in the dirt road. Horses grazed in an adjacent pasture."

From his secret perch David imagined he could watch people gathering around the house and barn, waiting for him to lead them on a mountain adventure; at night they would all return to the cabin to sit around the fire and talk about the day's events and what they'd learned.

"I used to spend a lot of time by myself reading out in the treehouse. And I'd imagine talking to all those people who had come from far away to learn from me. It was very vivid." He also imagined studying and preparing in order to have something good to share with them. He always felt completely in command of the situation.

"About this time, just when I was getting warmed up, I'd hear my mother calling me for dinner. I'd scurry into the house, the last one at the table, as usual."

"Romulus is going to found Rome and Remus is going into municipal bonds."

Recalling Your Own Childhood Dreams

Call the second main section in your notebook or computer: **Where Am I Going?** Label the first tab: *Childhood Dreams.*

Choose a time when it's quiet and you can be alone. Close your eyes and try to visualize the surroundings in which you most often used to dream. For example, when David pictured his treehouse on late summer afternoons, other memories flooded into his head.

Give yourself time to just sit and revisit your childhood. Then, in your notebook or computer, record as much as you can reconstruct of your dreams—what you imagined yourself doing when you grew up. When you were a child, nothing much stood between reality and your ideal future.

If you can't remember as much as you like, or you want to continue delving into your past imaginings, think back on all the people who knew you while you were growing up: parents, siblings, teachers, counselors, coaches, friends, neighbors, relatives, clergy, friends of your parents. On a sheet of paper, put down the heading: "People I Remember."

Make a list of literally everyone and anyone you remember. When the list is as long as you can make it, star those people you would most enjoy speaking with today. Then track them down. You may have to do some digging, but it's usually a tremendous pleasure to get in touch with people from your youth. Ask them the following questions and take notes on their responses.

- "In what field did you think I would end up working?"

- "Was there anything specific you imagined I'd be doing?"

- "Do you remember me talking about my dreams for when I grew up?"

You will probably want to tell them a little about why you are asking these questions. Chances are they will be curious. Peers may ask you to tell them what you thought they'd do too. All in all, you'll probably find this is a happy opportunity to get in touch with people whom you have not talked to in a while.

NEED CLUES?

- Did you have a favorite teacher? He or she would probably love to hear from you.
- Who was the adult, outside of the family, who had the greatest influence on you, whom you could locate now?
- Check messages written by your classmates in yearbooks. The messages themselves may contain valuable information, or may lead you to old friends whom it would be helpful to contact.
- Did you participate in special youth groups whose leaders might remember you?
- Was there any storekeeper you saw regularly who got to know you?
- How about your bosses from your childhood jobs?

When you talk with these people, be sure to record their comments, especially the ones that remind you of things you used to fantasize about.

Occasionally, people may remember things about you that feel foreign. Don't resist their comments, but do ask what they particularly remember that would illuminate their opinion. Our own memories have a way of being very selective.

To Sum Up

Recaptured childhood dreams are not the whole story. For one thing, they may be unrealistic in today's world. Or you may find that you're no longer as interested in them. But they may turn out to be important. The key is to discover how much meaning they hold for you now. We have a lot of evidence from our clients that childhood dreams offer powerful indications of future direction. In fact, people who try to

Your hobby is someone else's business; why not yours?

deny their dreams often find themselves haunted by them in indirect ways: lack of commitment to their work, for example, or lack of energy, psychosomatic problems, and frustration.

It's not that you will necessarily become the helicopter pilot or famous novelist that you dreamed about. But pursuing those old dreams can enrich your life in many other ways—in leisure and learning activities, for example, which re-engage interests that you set aside. Taking these up again may lead you into some related work that you haven't even considered yet.

In retelling the dreams that once mattered greatly to you, you have put a piece of the complex goals puzzle into place. You will find it enormously energizing to assemble the other pieces. For now, don't try to leap ahead to construct a definitive career goal or plan of action. Take it on faith that everything you will be doing in the coming chapters will shed light on the path ahead.

Interests and Fascinations

I N ADDITION TO your childhood fantasies, your current interests— especially those interests strong enough to be fascinations—will offer insight into a successful work life. When you are able to concentrate on what you enjoy or care deeply about, you have the energy needed to excel. The task here is to pay attention to as many of your true interests as possible so that you can incorporate them into your work.

People who jam all their interests and fascinations into their spare time can easily develop a resigned attitude toward life; this leads to an apathetic approach to work. These are not the movers and shakers whose stories inspire us to greatness.

COMING UP

A reintroduction to the things that interest you most.

☞ Read about people who matched jobs to their leisure interests.

☞ Learn how to identify and capitalize on your own interests.

Fortunately, hidden in your interests and favorite recreational pursuits are opportunities to earn good money—and enjoy doing it! You may wonder how leisure-time pleasures like "going to the beach" or "listening to rock music" could help you make a living. Take a look at the following examples of people who have built successful careers around personal enthusiasms that might seem frivolous at first glance.

Camping Out

Sam was an Air Force Lieutenant Colonel employed in the long-range planning department of NASA (National Aeronautics Space Administration). Part of his job was to dream up things that would be "nice to have," like a space station orbiting around Venus. He and his colleagues would then try to determine the feasibility and benefits of these ideas. As exciting as this was, Sam's true love was the great outdoors right here on earth. Almost every weekend he and his family went camping. In fact, although doing so didn't seem very practical, Sam secretly wished he could go camping for the rest of his life. "Oh, well," he would say, "you can't have everything."

Sam took a Crystal-Barkley course, which convinced him to at least try to find out if a career could be made out of his outdoor interests. First he contacted several camping manufacturers, two of them in Texas, a state where he and his family wanted to live. In his meetings with those who ran the firms, Sam discovered they were lacking a systematic way to develop and test new products. He wrote a proposal suggesting that he head up a new product development department. Naturally, to fully test the equipment Sam would have to go camping. His wife and kids would accompany him, since camping equipment is made for women and children too. One of the companies receiving Sam's proposal accepted it. And now, Sam is paid to think about and go camping. And if you find that a wild story, listen to this one.

Riding Roller Coasters

Would you ever think that someone who likes to visit amusement parks could make money doing it? Well, consider Gary. Ever since he took his first ride at age three, Gary loved roller coasters. Since that day, he has climbed aboard more than 30,000 amusement-park rides—all in the course of his work. How?

Unlike Sam, Gary always knew that he could make a living riding roller coasters, if he could just find the right angle. He never allowed "the system" or anyone in his life to deter him. On his vacations he traveled the country visiting amusement parks; he rated the rides in each park according to criteria he devised. He then wrote what turned out to be a bestselling book called *The Great American Amusement Parks.* Later he served as a location scout for the movie *Rollercoaster.* Where will Gary's fascination take him next? One thing he knows for sure—whatever the work, there will be a roller coaster somewhere in the picture.

Fishing

One well-known fishing membership association employs people to visit fishing sites in order to check out current conditions by fishing themselves. They report their opinions and then assist in setting up tournaments, which usually requires them to visit the sites again. Sounds just like a vacation!

Judging from these few examples, it is obvious that jobs can connect with your fascinations. Sometimes the job exists already, and sometimes you must invent it yourself. Either way, your interests and fascinations can become a part of your career. But first you need to fully understand them.

Uncovering Your Interests

In your notebook or computer, make a new tab called *Interests and Fascinations.* Begin to think about all the things that have attracted you lately. A movie? Something you read? Someone you met? A commercial on television? Even a billboard? Think about it. Let your mind run back over the last week or so. On a fresh page of your notebook, write down anything that has especially captured your attention recently.

Over the next few weeks, every time something piques your interest, make a note of it. If it's a magazine or newspaper article, clip it, and tuck it into your folder. Carry a little notepad with you; you can jot down notes, tear the pages out, and put them with your clippings. Include radio or TV programs, conversations, articles, movies—anything that lingers in your thoughts.

Be as specific as possible. You may be interested in business, but listing "business" is vague. Exactly what aspect of business interests you? (Management, sales, production, new products?) Write down your answer. What type of business? (Automobiles, communications, retail, restaurants, food processing and packaging?)

If "exercise" interests you, what kind of exercise? Where do you enjoy doing this exercise?

NEED CLUES?

- What are your favorite activities? Anything you enjoy qualifies as an interest, even if other people think it's unimportant or ridiculous. These are *your* interests.

- Have you read anything intriguing lately? Are there particular sections of newspapers or magazines you read regularly? What books have you bought, and why were you attracted to them?

- What courses or training seminars have you enjoyed? What topics did you like best? Perhaps you enjoyed getting hands-on experience with some equipment, carrying out projects, or learning something new.

- What movies or television programs have you seen that appealed to you? Think of the programs you watch regularly: news stories, specials, movies, sports, nature series.

- What do you like most about TV shows? If you enjoy nature programs because animals fascinate you, write down "wildlife"

as an interest. What kind of wildlife? Reptiles? Birds? Big cats? If you enjoy these programs because of the exotic scenery, write down "exotic settings" or be even more specific: "East Africa" or "Brazil."

- How do you like to spend your free time?

- If you had more time, what would you do with it?

- Can you think of a great conversation you've had with someone recently? Perhaps you got into an intense debate over an issue you feel strongly about. Or perhaps you enjoyed talking about a common topic of interest.

- Have you taken any trips recently? Think back to the places you visited and the people you met. What most caught your attention and enthusiasm? Even if you haven't been traveling, imagine the places you would like to go. What appeals to you about those places?

Interests can be discovered everywhere—at work, in leisure activities, around the dinner table, among family and friends. Be alert in capturing your interests and paying attention to all the aspects of your life in which these surface. Jot down new ideas as soon as you notice them.

Flashes of insight are like wild birds; unless you capture them, they fly away.

The idea is to develop a *long* list, without restrictions. Anything that interests you is worthy of mention, even if you don't believe it could ever relate to a career. Your list of interests is a dynamic document, so keep adding to it. In later chapters, your interests will help define your direction in work and life.

To Sum Up

By systematically delving into what captures your interests, you are assembling a rich array of possibilities for a rewarding career—a vibrant, creative life in which your work and non-work endeavors feel integrated. The process of systematically identifying your interests and fascinations lifts you out of the pattern of familiar or traditional expectations we and our families often establish for ourselves when, in truth, our interests may lie elsewhere.

Finding Direction

THE KEY TO finding a direction for your life is to discover and acknowledge what really matters to you. Easy to say, but by the time we're ready to think about such questions, society has usually made its mark on us. Legions of "shoulds" march through our consciousness, often camouflaging our true desires: "You should be more like your brother." "You should be making more money." "You should dress more conservatively." "You should go into your uncle's business." "You shouldn't work so hard." "You should work harder." "You should think about the future." "You should be spending more time with your family." With all of these mixed messages, no wonder it's hard

COMING UP

A window on what matters to you and what you really want. In this chapter you will:

☞ Undertake several fanciful activities designed to bring your inner desires to the surface.

☞ Find out where one of these activities took Elizabeth.

☞ Recognize the emerging themes that may help determine your goals.

to sort out what you really want for yourself. But if you don't, you'll never derive the kind of pleasure and satisfaction from your work that leads to real achievement.

Accessing What Matters

Chances are, much of what you think is important in life is buried beneath the surface. You have begun to explore some of this by recalling childhood dreams and pinpointing your interests, but there is more to it than that. The activities in this chapter are guaranteed to stimulate your thinking; for the time being don't worry about how you will use the results. Just enjoy whatever thoughts come to you. You will have plenty of time later to analyze what they mean to you.

Label a new tab or subhead: *What I Want.* All you need now is a pen and an open mind. Have fun!

Twenty Years From Now

Project yourself into the future. Imagine it is 20 years from today. You have just settled down for your morning coffee and opened the newspaper. There it is—your name in the headlines! Under the headline is a feature article about you. The story describes your accomplishments, where they took place, and what they meant to other people. It also includes quotations from you and your friends and colleagues.

"I think it's about time you got serious."

NEED CLUES?

- Newspaper readers expect dramatic headlines—"Jones Discovers Cure for Cancer," or "Jones Tops Bestseller List," or "Jones Among 500 Richest in America." Hot headlines are fine, if they reflect what you want to achieve in life. Your headline, however, may reflect a purely personal achievement and seem dramatic only to you: "Jones Helps Children Improve Reading Skills" or "Jones Promotes Zoning Plan to Protect City's Character."

- Elizabeth wrote "Gray's Books Bring the Past to Life" and David wrote "Goodman's Teaching Alters Corporate Culture."

- Although your headline might cover only one aspect of your accomplishments, feel free to include others in the story. In any case, be very detailed.

- At this point, don't worry if these accomplishments suggest that you might have to make fundamental changes in your life or if your own vision of your future varies substantially from what other people expect from you.

- Focus on *what* you have to say rather than how to say it. Don't worry about your writing style— just tell the story.

- This is no time to be modest!

At the top of a blank piece of paper write: "Twenty Years From Now," followed by the headline you envision.

Once you're satisfied with your headline, assume it has caught the attention of thousands of readers. Now, give them the story. Include in your article everything you want to be true in 20 years. Forget about being realistic or pragmatic. Dream, fantasize—write what you like. Take as much space as you wish.

When you have finished, enjoy rereading your story, then set it aside. Take a break before going on to the next activity.

The Billboard Exercise

Ready for another fantasy? Imagine learning that an enormous billboard, visible to everyone in town, is yours for a week. Normally the space is very expensive to rent, but this week it's free to you.

Now's your chance to send your most important message to your community. It might be a personal statement, a business announcement, or a philosophical message to the world. Obviously, it will need to be to the point, using words or pictures or both. Title this activity: "Billboard." Let your imagination have a field day.

NEED CLUES?

- Perhaps you have a cause you want to promote: protecting endangered species or feeding the hungry.
- Do you want to use the billboard to encourage people to do more or less of something (e.g., spend time with family or stop smoking)?
- You might want to promote some of your beliefs or values.

- Could your billboard advertise a service or product that might be yours in the future?
- David wrote "Green up our lives—more plants by the highway, at work, around town—everywhere!" Elizabeth wrote "No one can be free if anyone is oppressed. Support human rights for all."

Give yourself 10 or 15 minutes at the most to come up with your billboard. Doing this rapidly keeps you from trying to be too "sensible" about using this normally expensive space. When you are finished, tape your message to the wall to enjoy for a day or two.

One-Month Adventure

Let's move on to an imaginary adventure. Suppose you just picked up your mail. You see a letter from your Uncle Alan, who made a fortune in the contracting business. Uncle Alan always took a special interest in you, but you haven't heard from him in a while. What's he up to now, you wonder? You are thoroughly surprised when you read the letter.

"Dear Niece," he writes, "I've heard you're feeling a little uncertain about your place in the world. In my opinion, you need a refresher for mind and body. In hopes that you will return rarin' to go, I'm giving you an entire month, fully funded, to do anything you want, anywhere you want, with whomever you want. I will help you make the arrangements and secure whatever special equipment you might require."

What a concept! What's the catch? Only this: "All I ask is that you choose an activity that you think is *important and enjoyable*," Uncle Alan wrote. "Make sure it's *your* idea, not someone else's, and make it unrelated to your present job. Write me a letter explaining just how you plan to take me up on the offer. Give me all the details so I can be sure that you fully grasp the spirit of this adventure."

Well, let's play it out. Start by writing back to Uncle Alan, telling him all about your plans for a one-month adventure. For the moment, forget about the myriad reasons you can't do this: your deadlines at work, your sick mother, your kids, the mortgage payment. If you need more clues, take a look at the box on the next page. Store your letter under the heading: "One-Month Adventure."

Elizabeth's Adventure

After initially resisting thinking about anything as silly as a mythical uncle at a time when she was feeling completely stuck in her writing career, Elizabeth allowed her mind to drift to the possibilities. Silly, maybe, but what if? Here's the letter she wrote to "Uncle Alan."

It would be a treat to be in France again, in the middle of the Loire Valley for the month of October, when the grapes are being harvested. I would spend my time researching the stories behind medieval tapestries, taking the occasional day off from my research to join in the fun of the harvest, sampling new wine and old in the evening. I would stay with the Leclercs, a family I met years ago, who have a small manor house and vineyard outside of Tours. Their home would be a perfect headquarters, since they are also in the business of restoring tapestries, and through them I would gain access to some rarely visited chateaux and their tapestry collections.

I will spend each day at either a chateau or the University of Tours, which has an excellent department of medieval history and literature. I will pack a picnic each morning and head off into the golden light of autumn in my little rented car. My laptop computer will enable me to take notes on site. Each day at lunchtime, I'll find a different spot near the river or in a meadow, and spend two or three hours by myself simply enjoying my surroundings and my newly acquired knowledge. What heaven!

I will pass evenings with my old and new French friends, cooking together and spending long hours in conversation near the fire. My old friends are knowledgeable about medieval times and I am interested in their pursuits, so I will feel as if I am adding to my store of knowledge, which will enable me to share it with others.

NEED CLUES?

- If you plan to travel, prepare the itinerary. List the places you will visit, decide where you will be staying and for how long, outline your activities in each place. Be sure to include how you intend to travel: air, sea, rail.
- Provide enough detail to make your return letter interesting—even enticing—reading.
- Choose activities you know you would enjoy or have always dreamed of doing, but that are important to you.
- Part of your adventure could be an adventure in learning. And

perhaps it could include doing something for others.
- Skip any activities that are tied into an immediate problem. (If you are unemployed, you might want to use the month to find a job, but that isn't in the spirit of the adventure.)
- Money is no object; use as much as you need (but don't spend frivolously).
- Incorporate as many different people and activities in this adventure as you wish (but remember, you only have a month).

Making Sense of Fantasy

For the past few days, you have probably been musing over your responses to the activities in this chapter, perhaps wondering what thay all add up to. Now's the time to find out. Take your pages out of your notebook or printer or down from the wall, and place them side by side.

Make a fresh subhead: "What I Want—Themes." Read over your material and highlight the themes that jump out at you. You will recognize themes by the words or ideas that come up more than once. Write down every theme that seems to emerge from the exercises. It's fine to invite friends to peruse them with you.

You may want to list the themes in order of priority. Elizabeth noticed: "France, exotic countrysides, people who make me laugh, anything medieval, human rights, cooking."

Be sure to list all the themes you notice; you will refer to them again in the next chapter. Think about it: Have you left out anything important to you? Add it to your themes list now. Go back to Chapters 7 and 8 and note the themes appearing in your childhood dreams, interests, and fascinations.

To Sum Up

The thoughts and musings that occupy our daydreams or fantasies tell us much of what is true about ourselves. Often we fear paying attention to these or speaking out loud about them lest we appear naive or are accused of not dealing with reality. And we would seem unrealistic if we failed to reconcile our dreams with what is true for the

Fantasy furnishes the mind with rich alternatives.

people we want to interact with and the environment we want to operate in. The point of the Crystal-Barkley approach, however, is to make it possible to blend internal and external realities—to be who we are *and* to do good work for others.

So enjoy the thoughts that have come to you as the result of listening to your internal musings, knowing that by doing so you have greatly accentuated the positives of your future work.

Determining Your Goals

S ETTING GOALS FOR your
future can seem like a daunting
process. Questions like "What
do I want to accomplish with my life?"
or "What is my purpose on earth?"
loom so large. But it's easier to at least
begin to answer them now that you
have pertinent information about yourself at your fingertips. When you combine your ideas about what you want
to be doing and what you want to
achieve with your skills and values, you
can begin to articulate a direction for
your life: your goals. Goals are important because they help shape your life
and give it direction.

In the three previous chapters, you
learned important things about yourself while you were engaged in lighthearted activities. It's time now to step
back and analyze the material you have
gathered.

COMING UP

**A look at the themes
and patterns that
emerge from your
responses to earlier
activities and how
these relate to your
life goals.**

☞ Evaluate the meaning
of these themes in rela-
tion to the most impor-
tant areas of your life
(e.g., family, work, etc.).

☞ Bring all the elements
together in a coherent
statement that reflects the
genuine you.

☞ Gain a sense that
your prominent skills and
values are integrated with
your life's aspirations.

Goals Keep
You Going

Do you ever remember being stuck in a boring job? Or having a class in school you couldn't stand? Time passes slowly, even painfully. The clock on the wall reminds you just how long an hour can be. But when a task is connected to a larger goal, it suddenly becomes lighter, and time often passes almost unnoticed.

For example, an Olympic athlete might find his eyelids drooping hearing a lecture on muscular anatomy, but when he recognizes that the class contributes to his goal of succeeding in his sport, he regains alertness and does well in the class. The struggling entrepreneur who must reconcile his accounts once his staff has gone home each night does so willingly because he knows he's contributing to his larger goal of building a successful company with productive workers. The parent who wonders if her teenager will ever act like a human being musters the patience required because her goal is to nurture a fine person. You manage an extra 10 minutes on the step machine with your vision of a toned body before you. In other words, *goals keep you motivated and moving at the top of your form.*

Important Areas
of Your Life

Now is the time to review the themes that emerged in the previous three chapters. Get out your notebook and flip back to the work you did for Chapter 7, in which you recorded your recollections of your childhood dreams. You may also have spoken to people who remembered what you used to talk about when you were quite young. Make a note of the topics that appeared in your childhood dreams and any particular place or conditions that made up your image of where these took place. David, for instance, noted: "adventure," "presenting and learning," and "in the wilds." The goal is to pick out the highlights of what is most important to you in your childhood dreams.

Next, go back to Chapter 8 and review the long list of interests and fascinations you wrote. Do some fall into groups or relate to one par-

S.GROSS

ticular theme? Make a new list of the themes you see, and compare it to the themes that surfaced in Chapter 9, when you recorded your responses to "Twenty Years From Now," the "Billboard Exercise," and the "One-Month Adventure." You will probably see some similarities between the two lists. Merge them, listing themes in any order that seems right to you.

For each theme on the blended list, try to identify an area of your life that it might promote. Following are some ways of categorizing areas of life, but only you can know how to identify what's most important to you.

- Friends
- Family
- Business or professional activity
- Recreation
- Sports
- Cultural enjoyment
- Working
- Learning
- Loving

- Spiritual life
- Education
- Physical condition
- Community
- Money
- Home environment
- Music
- Staying healthy
- Financial security
- Nature

Make a new tab in your notebook or computer and label it *Important Areas of My Life,* and start writing down the areas that stand out in your life, using terms that are meaningful to you and leaving plenty of space under each heading. Then go on to see which themes correspond to them.

Themes may relate to more than one area of life. Elizabeth, for example, put *making people laugh* into both "Professional achievement" and "Recreation." She put *gourmet cooking* and *exotic countrysides* into "Recreation." When it came to her concern for *human rights,* she created a category that she called "Freedom." She put *women's issues* into "Freedom" and "Professional achievement."

Elizabeth went on to identify several more areas of life. Although there is no magic number, most people have between five and eight important areas of life.

Try to think of your areas of life—your goal areas—as an image. It doesn't matter if they suggest the five points of a star or the eight tentacles of an octopus; choose an image that speaks to you. Our clients have illustrated their goals with trees, engines, flowers, houses—all manner of images. Whether you choose to draw a picture and label the parts or simply to make a list, go on to describe what each area means to you in a sentence or two.

NEED CLUES?

- Do the areas of life you have identified cover all the types of activity you engage in? If not, add another area to your list (unless the activity is something that doesn't mean anything to you, in which case you may want to give it up).

- If you have always wanted to do something—compose music, travel around the world, start a business, or paint a picture—create an area of life that lets you embrace the endeavor. Give it a suitable name, such as "Cultural," "Entrepreneurial," or "Artistic."

- Don't let a current crisis in your life block your thinking. Just because you have pushed an area out of your life for now doesn't mean it should stay out. For instance, cultural pursuits may seem frivolous to you in the midst of a financial crisis, but engaging in inexpensive activities (reading a book or watching movies on videotape) may be exactly what you need to maintain your perspective.

Forming Your Goals Statement

L abel a new tab *Goals Statement.* When you feel you have identified all the important areas of your life, look over your list. Select the most immediately appealing. Say you choose "Friends." Write "Friends" at the top of a fresh sheet of paper or create a computer heading.

Now write down what you want to make happen in that area. You may want to make a number of things happen, so jot down as many notes as you wish. Consult the themes you recorded under this heading. When you have your thoughts together about "Friends," try to boil them down into one or two phrases that capture the spirit of what you want to make happen. Use action verbs with "ing" endings. That way you create goals that are not remote from you; you are living and working toward them.

Below are phrases that different people have used to explain what they wanted to make happen in the area of life they called "Friends."

- "Nurturing an ever-widening circle of friends, enjoying lots of good times together . . ."

- "Being an increasingly valued friend to a small circle of people who are special to me . . ."

- "Continually building friendships that are mutually supportive and educational . . ."

- "Maintaining lifelong friendships in which we take joy in one another's successes and receive comfort in times of grief . . ."

By clearly envisioning what you want to make happen in one important area of your life, you are beginning to articulate your goals. Do the same for your other areas of life one by one, until you have as many sheets of paper or headings as you have areas of life. Remember, these are *your* life goals; they will serve you throughout your life (not just for the next five years). As you gain more experience and self-knowledge, your goals may evolve, but their essential nature tends to remain the same. Therefore, you want your goals to feel big enough to last a lifetime. You may have an area of life called "Money." So, what do you want? "Making $100,000" won't last very long. (You don't want to have to do this exercise all over again!) A phrase like "Making enough money to live a comfortable life" can serve you forever.

Here are a few more examples of phrases different people used to describe common areas of life:

AREA OF LIFE	WHAT YOU WANT TO MAKE HAPPEN (GOALS)
Marriage and family	"Continually creating new ways to enrich my own life and the lives of the people I love best. . ."
	"Always 'being there' for my family . . ."
	"Raising and supporting my children in such a way that we all grow from the experience . . ."
Professional	"Always developing my skills and adding to my reputation as the best defense attorney in town . . ."
	"Singing and composing rock music that is popular with a broad-based audience . . ."
	"Playing an increasingly important role in space exploration, capitalizing on my research and analysis skills and interest by the unknown . . ."
Leisure time	"Taking great pleasure from running, tennis, and basketball . . ."
	"Enjoying good times at movies, community theater, and concerts . . ."
	"Regularly visiting and feeling renewed by the excitement of exotic places . . ."

Include Your Values and Skills

When you have written down your goal for each area of your life, begin weaving them together into a single compelling statement. Most people start with the goal area that seems most meaningful and try to end with their second most important goal, or a phrase that sums up their goals in an exciting way.

Within the goals statement, you may want to mention the skills and values that placed highest on your priority lists. If more than anything you want to be using your comedic skills, be sure to incorporate that

NEED CLUES?

- Goals are broad statements of direction, but they should also be very specific. Let's say you have an area of life called "Work." A goal of "Being happy" doesn't say much. Much more specific is "Continually feeling the exhilaration that comes from peak performance." Even better is "Continually feeling the exhilaration that comes from knowing that I'm performing surgery at the peak of my abilities."
- You may have been trained to set quantifiable goals: what, how much, when. At Crystal-Barkley we call these "objectives." For us, goals describe the mission—the long-range aspiration. Objectives tell the steps you will take to get there. Once you have goals for each area of your life, you will learn how to set objectives for each one.
- These are *your* goals; what other people think, even when well-intentioned, is irrelevant.
- Use *ing* verbs in goals statements to show that your life goals are ongoing.

in your goals statement. Or if you work best in the company of humorous, adventurous people, include that.

Here's a copy of David's goals statement to give you a clearer sense of how they read.

"I am feeling the thrill and adventure of breaking new barriers of learning and performance in my work managing and inspiring people, in my public speaking, and also in my explorations of the wilds; I am contributing to my own psychological and financial security and that of my loved ones; maintaining myself in the best physical shape possible for my age through diet and regular exercise; nurturing and feeling nurtured by the love I am giving to and receiving from my family, friends, and the greater community of which I am a part through my volunteer efforts; returning home to be refreshed by the beauty and order I create in my surroundings; ever feeding my need to know about people who are unlike me through reading and travel; and above all, feeling that I am a worthwhile citizen of the world."

By incorporating your goals into one statement—not several—you force yourself to integrate and connect. It may not be grammatically pristine, but this single-statement concept will help to keep you from pursuing incompatible aims. Many Crystal-Barkley clients have said, "Now I can see that I've been chasing after goals that are in conflict with each other."

To Sum Up

As beautifully as you can, letter your goals statement on a sturdy card and place it where you can see it every day. You will begin to notice subtle effects. You will make better decisions about how you use your time because you have a better sense of what you are all about.

In the end, we live our lives as we want. So the secret is truly knowing what we want.

Your goals statement completes a major step in the Crystal-Barkley process. However, let's not leave your future to chance. The rest of the process will show you how to bring about the life you envision for yourself.

Part Three

HOW DO I GET THERE?

Landing the job

Assembling a Plan of Action

B Y NOW YOU probably have a fairly clear picture in your mind of what you want to be doing with your life and how you want to be doing it. In this chapter you'll synthesize all the information you've gathered about yourself to date and turn it into a preliminary plan of action.

Call the third section of your notebook **How Do I Get There?** Label the next tab: *Assembling a Plan of Action.* At the top of a blank sheet of paper, write "Spontaneous Observations." Look back over the activities you've completed and write down any insights you have, such as: "The things I dreamed about as a child still fascinate me." Or, "I never realized how much I was attracted to new technological ideas." Or, "I must be a small organization kind of person." Keep adding insights as they occur to you. These thoughts are nuggets of the truth about you.

COMING UP

The beginnings of a plan for moving ahead with your life.

☞ Pull together the most important information you have learned about yourself to date.

☞ Create pictures and symbols that illustrate this information.

☞ Combine these pictures into a single image that represents a concrete framework for the steps that you will take from here.

Your next move is to create a dynamic plan of action—dynamic because it can be revised as you discover more about yourself. For this task you need to supply yourself with a large piece of posterboard, some colored pencils, and peel-off stickers (the removable kind).

Read through this chapter completely before starting your poster. It helps to have a sense of the whole project before you begin. Following are the elements that you will include in your plan of action poster. (You may place them anywhere you wish on the poster, but save a prominent spot for your goals statement.)

Super Skills. When you named your skill clusters in Chapter 5 you actually summarized much of "who you are." Plan to transfer these names to your poster in priority order under the heading "Super Skills," using a different colored pencil for each.

Your Likes and Dislikes. Choose an area on your poster that's large enough to accommodate three lists, those of your "likes" and "dislikes" for people, working conditions, and community. Starting with people, refer to your notes from Chapter 6 and write down those qualities you discovered you absolutely need under the heading, "People". If you have a priority order, use it. Do the same for dislikes, selecting the items you completely reject. Then, nearby, create similar lists under the headings "Working Conditions" and " Community."

Billboard. Take a look at that billboard you created in Chapter 9. Does its message still feel right to you? If not, revise it until you're satisfied. Transfer the slogan or artwork to your poster.

One-Month Adventure. Reread the letter you wrote to Uncle Alan in Chapter 9. What stands out about your proposed adventure? The lifestyle? A special interest? The people? What else? Write "One-Month Adventure" on your poster, and under it list these highlights.

Your Goals. Remember the card on which you wrote your goals statement? Take it out and copy it onto the most prominent place on your poster. Leave room around it to draw symbols that represent the different areas of your life. Or perhaps you will want to draw one main picture with elements in it reminding you of the many facets of your goals.

NEED CLUES?

- You may want to sketch your poster out before inking it.
- Your pictures don't need to be detailed; they simply need to speak to you. Sailing, for instance, could be depicted as a triangle and a line, or by a simple outline of a boat and sail.

- If you prefer, use magazine cutouts and make a collage rather than drawing images yourself.
- Artistic skills are not important. The poster is for you and you alone. As long as it's evocative of you, it has achieved its purpose.

This is an opportunity for you to revise your goals statement if you wish. If you need a refresher, turn to your work from Chapter 10 and reread "Areas of Life." Doodle a bit before you transfer your symbols to the poster. The idea is to create a visual reminder of your goals.

Does all this seem like child's play? Don't be misled. Remember how important images are in motivating us to achieve what matters to us; it's the seeing of the future that helps us to continue to work toward our goals. Your poster creates a lively visual reminder.

Putting It All Together

One of the benefits of creating your plan of action poster is that it often illuminates links between activities you thought were unrelated. David looked back over his activities in previous chapters and discovered that his "Billboard" tied in with two items on his "Interests" list and two items from his "Community Likes" list. Take a look.

Billboard: Green Up Our Lives! More Plants by the Highway, at Work, Around Town—Everywhere!

Interests: Beautiful country landscapes and gardens; Hiking in the woods.

Community Likes: Lots of trees and parks; natural wilderness within a short drive.

He realized for the first time that living and working close to nature must play a prominent part in his future choices. He began to draw a picture of a small house surrounded by a charming garden on his plan of action poster. Tall buildings were nearby but not right next to his house. He drew a road out through the mountains to even higher mountains, which somehow in the back of his mind seemed to represent not only the wilderness he loved, but also the future challenges he intended to build into his professional and recreational life. He then drew another picture of himself standing in a large room, talking to a few seated people. David's desired work environment and lifestyle were becoming an image of remarkable vividness.

Steps to Goals

At this point in the Crystal-Barkley process, specific, accomplishable steps that move you toward your goals often appear quite vividly in your mind. Add these images, which we'll call milestones, to your poster. David knew, for instance, that he absolutely had to have a house in the wilderness in his lifetime. He drew a cabin in the mountains, above his house outside of town. He wanted to be young enough to enjoy it, so he noted by it "Before my 45th birthday." Eventually, your plan of action poster will have many milestones noted on it; keep adding them, making this poster a current, attractive, and forceful reminder of what you are working toward, both long- and short-range.

Everyone's poster should include an entry along the lines of, "Make my next work decision by (date)." Examples of other specific steps clients have chosen are:

- "Putting aside sufficient money for my children's educations by (date)."
- "Securing my PhD in anthropology by (date)."
- "Buying a Ferrari by (date)."
- "Getting certified in scuba diving by (date)."

Clients have also included "maintenance" milestones, such as:

- "Maintaining my weight at no more than (number) pounds."
- "Exploring an unknown part of the world at least once every two years."
- "Visiting my mother at least once a month."

You can see from these examples that unlike your goals, which are likely bigger and probably more abstract, the steps you will take toward your goals are measurable and quantifiable. These are things you will do to make your goals real.

To Sum Up

When you have created your poster, it will be a colorful visual reminder of where you are headed and what you need to do to boost yourself along. Keep working on it until you have included all of the important information you have learned about yourself and your direction so far. Leave

> *If it's clear in your mind's eye, you are likely to achieve it.*

some open space so that you can make additions as you learn more about your ideas. Your research, or survey plan, which we'll discuss next, will become an essential part of your overall plan.

Your poster can also become a great conversation piece if you choose to let other people see it. It will stimulate your own actions and the interest and help of others as well.

Making a Survey Plan

COMING UP

A look at how to conduct a successful survey. You will:

☞ Choose a clear and specific topic to survey.

☞ Learn how to find the people who will be the best sources of information for you.

☞ Develop the right questions to ask.

O BVIOUSLY, DISCOVERING WHO you are and what you want and need from life is a great accomplishment, but still it is only part of the Crystal-Barkley equation. The balance lies in discovering what employers need and want and how this corresponds with what you have to offer. To this end, we introduce "surveying," a research technique through which you will ultimately match your needs and desires to the needs of people who will pay for your services. It involves systematically exploring a topic of interest to you, primarily by meeting people who know about the subject.

Once learned, surveying becomes a way of life; the more you do it, the better you get at uncovering exactly the information you need to focus your interests and pick out your next job. You can also use surveying for every kind of personal decision-making, including buying expensive items, planning vacations, solving medical problems, and developing hobbies. Surveying is enjoyable because it is based on your personal interests.

The purpose of surveying is to gather information; it frees you of the burden of trying to second-guess or impress a potential employer or of making an immediate decision, whether about a job or anything else. Thus, surveying is much less stressful than a typical job interview. In fact, many of our clients find surveying very enjoyable.

From an Interest to a Survey

Let's take a look at how one of our clients, Steve, turned his interest in the computerization of the publishing industry into a survey. More than a decade ago, before computers had infiltrated every aspect of business, Steve was pondering how to further his career in publishing, and was trying to figure out whether he needed an advanced degree in communications. He was working as a reporter for a magazine, but his skill clusters showed that his biggest talents lay in his grasp of technology and his ability to teach others. After analyzing his plan of action poster, he realized that he was interested in exploring the computer systems required to run a large publishing company. Steve also recognized that he eventually wanted to be one of the people at the top who made the decisions that shaped the direction of an organization. Was becoming an expert in computer systems a viable route to achieving this goal? He felt he didn't know enough to make a good decision. It was time to survey.

Developing a Survey Plan

The apparent subject of Steve's survey was computer applications in the publishing world, but that topic seemed too broad. More specifically, he wanted to learn how computer systems might give publishers of monthly and weekly magazines a competitive edge in efficiency, flexibility, and bottom-line costs, and what role he could play in the process. To this end, he developed a survey plan. Follow along with Steve and you will learn how to write out your own plan. Putting a plan on paper and becoming clear about what you hope to achieve is always the first step of surveying.

Survey Subject: Magazine publishing computer systems.

Survey Objective: To discover the degree to which top management, those in charge of present magazine systems, and leading technological developers feel that computer systems will drive the publishing industry in the future.

Steve wanted this information in time to make a decision about graduate school. He gave himself 30 days in which to speak to at least five people in each of three categories: management, systems managers, and software and hardware developers.

"If we're so smart, how come we're not rich?"

WHO TO SEE—AND WHEN

There are three categories of people to see when you're surveying. They are:

- **Third parties** are people who know a lot about, but aren't directly involved in, the field or industry of your survey. These often include journalists, consultants, and people who run the professional associations or agencies that regulate industries.
- **Users or Buyers** are the people who use or buy the products or services that interest you.
- **Providers** are those who are manufacturing the product or providing the service. Often these are the people whom you ultimately want to work for or with.

For example, suppose you were surveying to determine the best stereo system for a 400-square-foot loft space. In this case, third parties might include reviewers for specialty audio magazines, acoustical engineers, and vocal artists. Users or buyers would be the loft owners who have such stereo equipment. And providers would be the manufacturers who make and the salespeople who sell such equipment.

Let's look at another example. Suppose you were looking into providing home medical services to the elderly. Excellent third-party sources would include the various associations that represent medical service providers and the official bureaus that regulate them. Users would be the individuals who use the services and their families. Local hospitals and other health care agencies would be among the providers.

It's important to recognize who occupies which category because the order in which you see people matters. It's usually best to meet with third-party sources first, as it's unlikely you will ever approach them for a job. It's easier to relax with them and you'll be honing your survey skills while you're collecting information.

Generally, users or buyers will be your next stop. They can give you an entirely new perspective on your survey subject because they know whether the benefits touted prove to be true, whether there are wear or service problems, and whether they would make the same purchase again. No one is as eager to talk as the owner or user of a new product or service. Try to include those with enough experience to discover problems.

Providers are your last stop. They can provide insight into the needs, hopes, and problems they are dealing with, any one of which could be tailor-made for your skills and goals. Remember, even though providers are more likely than third parties to be the people you'll want to work for, surveying meetings are not job interviews. At this stage, your objectives are to establish rapport, gather information, and make contacts. Based on your visits with many people during surveying, you will later decide on your top choices of employers.

How do you find all these people? Do some background reading. You will likely come across many names of people who could shed light on your subject. Also try brainstorming with friends and family. Play the "Who do you know?" and "Who do you know who knows someone who might know?" game. Most surveyors end up with more people on their list than they could ever find time to see.

Location of Survey: Steve confined his survey to a 50-mile radius.

Sources of Information: Some obvious sources were right in Steve's own company. He listed the production managers and top management at his magazine and at other magazines inside and outside the parent company. He also listed the hardware and software developers who supplied these magazines.

In thinking about where to find these developers, Steve remembered some other important sources of information: the people who write about publishing and technology development for industry magazines. He decided to make trips to the public library, the library at a nearby university, and the downtown business library, where he checked the periodical index, read articles, searched the on-line services and looked for names of people to call. He also uncovered the names of professors who taught in related fields at the university. Gathering enough sources of information turned out to be fairly easy.

You too will want to do background reading before going to talk with people in person. It is important not to lose precious time when visiting people by getting answers to questions that you could have easily found on your own. Instead, be prepared, as Steve was, to briefly display current knowledge about your interest and the work of the person you are seeing. They'll be favorably impressed and you will be much more comfortable.

Questions to Be Answered: With many busy people to see, Steve knew he had to have his questions ready. He didn't want to waste anyone's time fumbling around, so he developed his list of questions in advance. All of these would be tailored to the specific person responding, but outlining them gave him an overall picture of what he wanted to learn.

■ "What are the major changes you have observed or dealt with in publishing technology?"

■ "To what extent do you feel you were prepared to deal with this?"

■ "Have you encountered resistance to the new developments?"

■ "How have you dealt with it?"

■ "How much of a role do you feel technological advances will play in the direction and growth of publishing in the future?"

■ "What role do you envision systems experts playing in top management in the future?"

■ "What advances do you see coming down the road, with respect to publishing systems?"

■ "What has happened in your day-to-day dealings to make you most aware of the impact of computers on the future of publishing?"

■ "What type of educational or work experiences would you recommend to someone intending to become expert in selecting and installing leading-edge systems in a magazine publishing house?"

■ "How much do the opinions and knowledge of technology vary between the top brass and the workers in publishing houses?"

■ "How do you think the issue of worker protection and unions can be dealt with most fairly in the face of technological advances?"

■ "What do you think is the realistic long-term earning potential for someone heading up systems for a major magazine?"

■ "What about at the systems manager level?"

Despite all his preparation, Steve felt nervous about starting his survey, so he decided to practice on a subject totally unrelated to his work interests. He chose white-water canoe trips. He refined his subject to "day-long white-water canoe trips with a guide in the mid-Atlantic region." Steve spent a weekend on this survey, and found that *when two people are interested in the same subject, the information flows.*

He asked around his racquetball club and discovered two people who were white-water enthusiasts. He also called a camp counselor he had been close to in his youth who was very pleased to hear from him and immediately told him about someone who had written a guide for white-water day trips. With a bit of search-

Luck favors the prepared mind.

ing, Steve found the guide and read it avidly; then he called its author. It turned out that the author was going to be visiting nearby, and they set up a time to meet. What luck!

Steve felt very relaxed doing his practice survey and wanted to maintain that feeling for his technology survey. In order to add to his confidence, he decided to role-play the technology survey with a friend.

Steve asked the friend to play the role of a university professor. The "professor" needed no special expertise for the part, only a willingness to behave with a professorial demeanor.

Role-playing was difficult at the beginning; Steve felt somewhat foolish. But when he'd gotten through a couple of role-plays with his friend, he discovered he was relaxing a lot more. His friend even began to get interested in the subject.

Steve spent a weekend catching up on his background reading. He then thought specifically about how he would approach the various people with whom he planned to talk. He found he could introduce himself smoothly by drawing directly from his survey objective. You'll find you're able to fashion similar introductions when you're clear about your survey objective.

Steve started his survey at his own magazine, talking casually to systems people working around him. One of Steve's opening gambits went like this: "I've watched you install the new production system here and I'm fascinated with what all of this means. I'd like to hear your take on it. Would you join me for lunch on Thursday, so we could talk about it?" He found it easy to expand his efforts from there. In fact, every-

HOW TO MAKE YOUR SURVEY WORK

Here's how to plan a good survey:

1. Decide on the subject that most intrigues you.

2. Refine and focus that subject into a specific topic by asking yourself (several times) *exactly* what it is about that subject that interests you so much.

3. Turn your specific topic into a *survey objective* by setting standards for completion. Include the kind of background research you'll do, the type and number of people you will talk with, where you'll undertake the survey, and by when it will be completed.

4. Brainstorm alone and with friends and family all possible sources of information: print, video and on-line sources, as well as people.

5. Do your background research first, but don't get stuck there.

6. Formulate your questions.

7. Practice on a less important subject; choose anything that interests you, but make sure it's a subject totally unrelated to your employment search.

8. Role-play the survey with a friend. First, you play the role of the person surveying; then role-play again, reversing roles so that you get a feeling for what the people you'll see will be experiencing.

9. Get busy seeing people; relax as much as you can; have fun!

10. Keep good records. Either take notes during your meetings or right after.

11. Write notes thanking people for their time and information.

where he went he seemed to find someone who knew about the subject, or someone who knew someone who did. Steve made an important discovery early in his survey: *When your conversation is based on a genuine interest and not on getting a job, people are almost always forthcoming.* By taking some action on his survey every day, Steve was able to gather more than enough information in 30 days to start making decisions important to his future work. He realized that the best place to learn was most likely on the job. He decided to look for an assistant systems manager position and, at the same time, to bolster his knowledge by enrolling in an evening course.

Planning Your Survey

Go through exactly the same steps as Steve did. (For a quick overview of the survey process, see "How to Make Your Survey Work," page 105.) First, determine your survey subject. This will come directly from the information you have gathered about yourself previously and will be represented on your plan of action poster. You may decide that you want to look into more than one subject. That's fine. But start with the one that most appeals to you. Once you're done, if you still want to, go on the next.

You don't want this process to be open-ended, so set yourself a schedule with an end point. Determine your timetable by deciding when you want to have made a change in your work, then work back from that date. Make sure you allow yourself a reasonable amount of time to survey.

Write out your survey plan in your notebook or computer. Writing it out forces you to focus and clarify your thoughts. And do your background reading. You don't want to be caught short, feeling you should have known some obvious fact about your subject. Plus, background research prepares you for fruitful conversations and even lets you bring useful information to the people you are seeing. Consider starting with a "practice survey," as Steve did. Choose a subject related to a recreational activity or some other lighthearted interest that's not work-related. Practicing gives you a chance to get comfortable with the technique before you start talking with people who could affect your future. Role-playing with a friend also helps build your confidence so you will come across in a relaxed, comfortable way during the real

NEED CLUES?

- Every question needn't be asked of every person.
- More questions will surface as you research library literature and speak with people.
- Review your questions. If a question doesn't directly target

some aspect of your survey objective, drop it. (This is an important standard to keep you on track.) If an unrelated question feels absolutely necessary to you, you may need to alter your survey objective.

thing. All this preparation helps make surveying the two-way street that all good conversations are.

Pay particular attention to devising pertinent questions (Chapter 14 will help in this process), and role-play your delivery of these. This is no time to shoot from the hip. Your working future depends on it.

To Sum Up

Surveying is the art of gathering specific, relevant information on a subject of genuine interest to you in order to make informed decisions about your future. This is done primarily on a firsthand basis— that is, by meeting with people in person.

Surveying is *never* about a job; if it were, you'd probably get marched right down to the human resources department before you even know if you're interested in working for that organization, let alone in what kind of job. To survey well, you must believe that you are entitled to information before making decisions. And you must value yourself enough to put in the necessary effort to acquire information.

Surveying produces three important results: rapport, information, and contacts. Of these, rapport is the most important. It is your ability to establish rapport that makes the information flow and makes people want to recommend you to other contacts. People like to talk about their interests; they like to talk about what matters to them. When their interests match your own, you've got a recipe for a stimulating, dynamic conversation.

Effective Introductions

S O, YOU'VE MADE your survey plan, done your background research, and you're ready to set up your first meeting. If you're trying to set up an appointment with a stranger, you'll need to introduce yourself in such a way that the person you're talking to will quickly understand who you are and why you want to speak with him or her. Plus, you must make the person *want* to speak with you.

Telephone calls and letters are the way we usually introduce ourselves to professionals. Most of us are nervous about approaching strangers in business, so we look for the most standard, inoffensive manner of introducing ourselves. Such innocuous techniques serve us least well because we end up sounding like everyone else or, even worse, like nobody at all. Fortunately, you can present yourself as a unique individual and also adhere to certain basic rules of professional courtesy. Read on to find out how.

COMING UP

Ways to make the most of your initial approach to a contact you don't know.

☞ Refine and polish your unique message.

☞ Rehearse possible telephone scripts.

☞ Write a convincing and interesting letter, whether you are asking for a meeting or requesting information.

Making Contact

M aking introductions by telephone and letter comes naturally to some people, but it is also a skill that can be learned. Your objective is to make your introduction so appealing and so easily understood that your interviewees will be not only willing but eager to meet with you. A well-received introduction sets the stage for a meeting that's rewarding and productive for both of you.

By and large the personal approach—a face-to-face meeting or telephoning—is the most effective way to introduce yourself. Our rule of thumb is to introduce yourself in person or with a phone call first and then follow up in a day or two with a letter. Letters are useful; they demonstrate your ability to communicate clearly and to follow through on your actions. But they are best read against the backdrop of the personal rapport established in conversation. It takes confidence to

NEED CLUES?

- Do your background reading thoroughly. Being well-grounded in the subject gives you needed confidence and helps you to stay focused during the conversation.

- Continually evaluate your comfort level with your survey subject and the people you are seeing. If it feels good, you may be a natural for the field; if it doesn't, you may want to rethink your direction.

- Before making your first call, practice; ask a friend to play the part of the person you're calling.

- Make a script or an outline and read it aloud several times before the call to be sure you sound natural. Then, put the script away before the call so you're sure to listen to what the other

person is saying and are fully engaged in the conversation.

- Be prepared to give receptionists or assistants a concise explanation of why you are calling. Try to strike up a friendly, brief conversation with them; the people who answer the phone can help you or stand in your way.

- Have your pen and calendar handly when you make the call. It's deadly to say "Hold on a second while I get a pencil." And, if necessary, don't forget to get directions.

- Persistence is the key to making successful contacts by telephone. If you can't reach someone, try, try, and try again. Remember, it's not you the person is rejecting. He or she doesn't even know you!

make this sequence of contacts work. And confidence comes from three things: knowing what you want to say, having enthusiasm for the subject, and practice.

The person receiving your telephone call, letter, or visit needs to know who you are, why you are calling, and what you want him or her to do for you—or vice versa. If you remember these three needs, you will usually get a fair hearing, and you may get much more than that.

It's important to tell enough about yourself and what you wish to accomplish to assure the person that yours is not a frivolous request—and that you have real

The eloquent expression of genuine interest creates a memorable impression.

enthusiasm for the subject at hand. To carry this off, you must have done enough thinking about your topic that you already have some ideas about what you might do with the information you are gathering. You've probably had the experience of speaking with someone who had no idea how he could follow up on what he was asking about. Such conversations feel like a waste of time.

However, when two people share an interest and information is exchanged, there is always profit to both parties. Even though you are the surveyor, you will still have information to give to the person with whom you are meeting. For example, while you were doing your background research you may have come upon an article that would interest the person you're meeting with that he or she may have missed. You may actually be more knowledgeable about the competition's recent activities or new trends or technological developments than he or she is. It may turn out that your visit is as informative and valuable to the interviewee as it is to you.

Let's assume that you have assembled a list of the people with whom you would like to speak, and you've practiced introducing yourself to a friend in a couple of role-plays. You're ready to start meeting the people on your list. Go ahead—pick up the telephone and call (or, if it's possible, arrange to bump into) the first person on your list. Start with the person who feels most familiar or approachable to you. The more you do it, the more natural introducing yourself and your topic will become.

Examples of Telephone Scripts

In the following examples, notice how the surveyors explain their specific topics while they are telling who they are and why they are calling.

Give your name.	Hello, Mr. Baldwin. My name is Sean Baker.
Explain why you are calling.	Elaine Thomas suggested I give you a call about the special-effects work you do.
Say something genuinely flattering.	I saw the Jupiter exploration film you and she made last fall and found it amazing, especially the technical side of it.
Tell about yourself and what the person can do for you.	I am a software developer looking into creating a program that produces special effects for science films—particularly in simulating explosions. This has become a genuine fascination of mine and I wonder if we might put our heads together briefly.
Set the time and restate it.	How would next Thursday at 11:00 be for you? Fine, I'll be at your office at 11:00 on Thursday. You're on the fifth floor, right?

Or, consider this example.

Give your name.	Hello, Ms. Stoddart. This is Christina Levitt.
Explain why you are calling.	I read in *Outside* magazine about the new camping equipment you're getting ready to market, and I was hoping I could take a few minutes of your time to discuss this.
Say something genuinely flattering.	I was very impressed with the amount of rigorous testing you give your equipment.
Tell about yourself and what the person can do for you.	As someone who leads cold-weather hiking groups, I am continually experimenting with new ways to keep warm. I would very much enjoy spending a few minutes to learn whether you think the materials and combinations I am using are the best ones to suggest to my clients.
Set the time and restate it.	Would Wednesday at 2:00 be good for you? Then, what day might be better? Great, Friday at 5:00 it is. Where would you like to meet? Good, I'll be there at 5:00 Friday afternoon. Thank you.

If you have a tough time getting through to someone, don't take it personally. Understandably enough, busy people may not make a stranger's call a high priority. For the time being, go on to someone else. But do call back again; persistence does produce results. And if you simply cannot get beyond the receptionist or assistant, resort to introducing yourself by letter.

Effective Letters

Good letter-writing takes practice and unfortunately, most of us these days are out of practice. Following the few simple rules outlined below, however, will help you to present yourself appropriately and convincingly, whether you're writing a letter of introduction, a thank-you note, or a proposal (these last letters are dealt with in Chapter 16).

The number-one requirement for writing a good letter is to be enthusiastic. Fortunately, you already have the number-one ingredient. You are writing this letter because you *want* to.

Rules for All Letters

■ Begin with "Your reputation as," "It was good of you," or *any* beginning which puts the letter in the recipient's context. Do not mention yourself first; never begin a letter with "I."

■ Make sure your letter is at least three paragraphs long.

■ Use white, buff, or gray paper, 8½-by-11 inches, unless your letter is intended as an informal response to an informal meeting, in which case you could use smaller paper or a correspondence card.

■ Your name, address and telephone number should be typed, printed, or engraved at the top center of the first sheet in black, gray, maroon, navy, or dark green, or typed at the lower left of the letter. Business or professionally directed letters are not the place to demonstrate flamboyance.

■ Always put your return address on your envelopes.

■ Never use a standard-format letter; each letter should be composed so that it could only be to that particular recipient.

Letters of Introduction

Letters of introduction should include the same information as telephone introductions, but not in the same order. Normally, the best order is: 1) Something genuinely flattering about the recipient and his or her work. 2) Who you are. 3) What you want—or why you are writing. 4) The time and method for further contact. 5) An expression of thanks for the attention given to your request. Take a look at the following two examples:

BERTRAM V. DILLARD
125 EAST RIVER AVENUE
PEABODY, MA 01960

April 14, 1995

Dr. Sarah Myers
Director of Interior Design
Evans-Lowell Corporation
1402 North Village Avenue
Rockville Centre, NY 11570

Dear Dr. Myers,

Your article in last month's Interior Design Review has been the topic of much discussion in my office these past few weeks. Your ideas on the Newcomb Technique are, to my mind, revolutionary and have stimulated me to try to learn more about the effect of color on productivity in office environments.

I'm an architect with the firm of Haswell, James and Sullivan in Peabody, Massachusetts. My specialty is renovating existing workspaces. My purpose in writing to you is to ask if you could provide me with some further information that could help me launch my research.

Would you be able to speak with me for a few minutes by phone sometime at your convenience? I will call you within the next few days to see about setting up an appointment. I very much appreciate your consideration of this request. I'm sure you'll be able to head me in the right direction.

Cordially,

Bertram V. Dillard
Bertram V. Dillard

SALLY LEE TREADWELL
22-B CIRCLE COURT
NEW ORLEANS, LA 70112

March 16, 1995

Professor Jack Marks
Department of Computer Science
317 Stetson Hall
University of North Carolina
Raleigh, NC 27602

Dear Professor Marks,

Our mutual friend Professor Paul Cox told me about your work and suggested that I write to you. I am a computer science major who will graduate in June, and I'd like to move to the Raleigh-Durham area sometime this summer. I'm currently researching software developers in the area, and am hoping you could provide me with some information.

I took Professor Cox's basic programming class as a sophomore and am now doing an independent study under his supervision. My project involves writing a program that small retail businesses can use to track inventory. I'm hoping to go on to use my programming skills in a job at a small, innovative software development company in the Raleigh-Durham area. Professor Cox thought that through your work with the university you might have come into contact with many of the software developers in the area and could help me determine which ones to approach.

I plan to be in Raleigh during my spring break, from April 8th through the 16th. Would it be possible for me to stop by your office to discuss all this? I will call you in a few days about setting up an appointment. I know you are a busy man, and promise to keep our meeting brief and to the point.

Thanks in advance for your consideration of my request.

Best wishes,

Sally L. Treadwell

Sally L. Treadwell

To Sum Up

The investment you make in learning to introduce yourself in person, by phone, and in writing will serve you well for the rest of your life. Introductions enable you to announce the quality of your work in advance and to create a favorable impression that lingers afterward. They get you in the door—and help get you invited back later.

More About Surveying

B Y THIS TIME you have had a chance to get started with your surveying. You have probably found that some research goes smoothly and productively and some efforts founder. In this chapter you'll learn how to further develop your survey technique and expand its scope and productivity. You'll also learn what to do if surveying reveals that you're not as interested in the field as you thought.

While you've surveying, it helps to remember these two principles: The more information you have, the better your decisions will be. And you are responsible for gathering your own information.

Only after you've fully researched your own interests and needs, as well as those of potential employers, should you turn to the task you've been working toward—developing proposals for the people you'd like to work for.

COMING UP

How to develop an even more sophisticated and successful surveying technique.

☞ Make sure that your survey is leading you to potential employers and giving you insights into their needs.

☞ Learn surveying etiquette and the impact of your personal style on other people.

☞ Find out more about how to ask the most productive questions.

☞ Learn how to organize and evaluate the information you have gathered.

Elizabeth's Survey

Elizabeth arrived at a topic and a survey plan based on one of her primary interests—medieval history and art. She had an idea that she could present the medieval period in a new and much hipper fashion than is normally the case. She wondered if there were any interest in visually lush books that conveyed medieval history in the style of a novel. She remembered reading Anya Seton's novels and immediately images of the kind of books she'd like to do came to mind.

Elizabeth knew of one publisher who had republished several children's fairy tales with beautiful art works as illustrations. She wondered if they had considered using medieval art for their books.

Elizabeth honed her interest into a specific topic: Determine the existence of and interest in vividly retold medieval stories and history, gorgeously illustrated with reproductions of original works of art. Given her skills and longtime interests, the topic seemed like a natural. She wondered why she had never thought of it before. The fact is that Elizabeth had re-met herself through revisiting some of her fantasies as she worked through the Crystal-Barkley process.

She decided to learn everything she could about her subject within six weeks by talking with at least five medieval art experts, five bookstore managers specializing in either art books or children's books, three museum curators of medieval art, five book editors, and three literary agents. She planned to prepare by doing a thorough search of what was currently on the market as well as what was written about it at the midtown library. She already had a lot of notes and books related to the subject, so in a sense she had a head start. In fact, when Elizabeth went through her own materials, she discovered she could put several names of people she already knew on her initial list of people to contact.

In spite of her familiarity with the subject, Elizabeth was a little nervous when it came to setting up her first meetings. After a few approaches, however, she could see that the process was working and she began to relax. By the time she called the tenth person on her list, a historian at Yale whom she had read about in her library research and from whom she hoped to learn more about some of the stories she wanted to tell, she felt as though she were making contact with an old friend. Her conversation went like this:

> *Secretary:* Good morning. Dr. Waltham's office.
>
> *Elizabeth:* Is Dr. Waltham in? I'm calling to speak with him about his latest research regarding medieval families of southwestern France.
>
> *Secretary:* Are you a student?
>
> *Elizabeth:* No, I wish I were. I am a writer and researcher myself. I would love about 10 minutes of Dr. Waltham's time to round out my research, and I may be able to tell him some things I have discovered that relate to his work.
>
> *Secretary:* Just a moment. I'll see if he's available.
>
> *Dr. Waltham:* Hello, this is Eric Waltham. What can I do for you?

This is what Elizabeth had to say about her conversation with Dr. Waltham: "From then on, I was on a roll. I simply told him what I was trying to do and he was happy to respond. He suggested I come up to Yale and sit in on one of his lectures the following week, and said we could chat afterward.

"I made a point of arriving early so I could stop in the Yale Library and check out any references to Dr. Waltham's work that I might have missed. Then I went over to his office and spoke to the secretary who had answered the phone when I called. I thought it might come in handy to know her better in case I wanted to call Dr. Waltham again.

"During the lecture, Dr. Waltham referred to parallels between medieval and contemporary society. That gave me a jump-off point for our conversation. As it turned out, we had such a good time talking about our hopes and frustrations in making the medieval period accessible to a broad public audience that I had to remind him that he had said he had another appointment. He left me with the names of several people in publishing whom he thought might be interested in my ideas. And I promised to send him photographs of some particularly illustrative tapestries of the area he was currently concentrating on. I knew I had made a new professional friend."

Elizabeth's experience is typical of most surveys. Sometimes, however, surveying reveals that the topic you believed to be so compelling really isn't as interesting as you thought. You may find that a different aspect of the specific topic is more interesting. For instance, after making his plan of action poster, David decided that he wanted to use his teaching and presenting skills working with bright, motivated, professional people. He thought he'd do best by starting his own consulting company and doing corporate-sponsored training sessions at company sites within the greater Los Angeles area. But his background reading and early meetings with people who had participated in this kind of training meetings convinced him that the corporate environment was too distracting to achieve the level of learning that he wanted to engage in when leading groups. In addition, he realized that he wanted to work as well as live closer to nature. He altered his survey objective to focus on genuinely transformational corporate training programs being carried out at remote sites in California, Arizona, Nevada, and Oregon.

Occasionally you may lose interest in your survey subject altogether when you get a firsthand look at it. You may not like the type of people you meet, the environment, the tempo of the work, or some other reality of that field. If this happens, rethink your specific survey objective. Why did you choose this topic to begin with? Are there other fields or aspects of the one you chose that make use of your skills and better match your values? Can you redirect your survey? The advantage of surveying is that it enables you to gather the information necessary to make decisions you can live with happily. If the survey reveals that you really don't like the particular field you're investigating, then it's saved you months, possibly years, of unhappiness.

Surveying for Opportunities

When you first begin surveying, your goal will likely be to determine whether the particular career path you've chosen is truly for you. You'll want to find out whether you'll be challenged, your top skills will be used, the people are collegial, and so on.

As you get further into the survey, your focus should widen. In addition to researching the above, you should be trying to identify potential employers and to determine their needs. Ideally, by the time you complete your survey, you should have a number of potential employ-

120

ers in mind. This expansion of focus may occur naturally. David, for instance, set up a meeting with the owner of a corporate training firm called Creative Learning and immediately hit it off with the owner. Even though Davis originally set up the meeting to find out about starting his own independent firm, the rapport that he established led him to consider an in-house position there. This happened because David learned that the firm's work was just the kind he wanted to do.

Because she chose to approach only those book editors whom she knew were interested in beautifully illustrated books, Elizabeth also found that she naturally came into contact with potential employers.

"I changed my mind. I'd rather be a big enchanted prince in a small pond, rather than a small enchanted prince in a big pond."

The purpose of her initial meetings was not to find a job, but rather to determine the potential market for books on the medieval period. Nonetheless, during the course of her conversations she developed a relationship with the editors that made it easy to approach them when the time came to propose a job.

Our client Steve, who, as you probably remember from Chapter 12, was trying to get involved in systems management for magazines, had to make a specific point to meet with potential employers. He feared that his own company would be reluctant to "demote" him to assistant systems manager, so he had to seek out other possible employers as well.

A word of warning: Remind yourself that surveying is not the time to discuss a job. Your goal is to find out whether the organizations you're visiting seem appealing and whether they appear to have a need for your skills, not to get yourself hired. That comes later in the process, once you've determined that they are attractive potential employers and have needs you are equipped to fill. Then you will develop proposals outlining what you can do for them.

Meeting Etiquette

Your behavior and attitude during surveys determine whether people want to talk with you. People like to talk to people with whom they feel comfortable and share a mutual interest. You've already got a shared interest. Your dress and speech, your enthusiasm, your listening skills and body language, your promptness, and your appreciation are all important too.

Plan to be a little early for meetings. You can use the extra time to compose yourself, observe, and learn from the surroundings. When greeting people, always use their names and remember the old adage about a firm handshake being the best handshake.

Do not call a person substantially older than you by his or her first name, unless invited to do so—then *be sure* to use it.

When entering someone's office, wait to take a seat until you are invited or until the person you are visiting is seated. To do this is not only polite: If you are too quick, you might upset the other person's anticipated seating arrangement.

DRESSING FOR SURVEYING

While you're doing your background research try to figure out how the people you will be visiting are likely to be dressed, and for the survey meeting adjust your own dress code to match theirs. This may mean wearing clothes or styling your hair in a way you don't feel comfortable with, but that's simply what you've got to do. If you want people to open up to you, you must make them feel you are one of them. For example, a graphics designer would be uncomfortable if you came in wearing a business suit, but a mortgage banker would expect it. If in doubt about dress, lean toward the conservative side.

No matter what style of dress you choose, make meticulous grooming a habit and be certain that all leather accessories—shoes, handbags, briefcases—are in tip-top shape.

Accessorize simply. Excessive jewelry is distracting. A watch or one bracelet (with nothing jangling off it) is sufficient. Avoid big stones.

Never smoke, and never ask if you may smoke. Since we're rapidly evolving to a no-smoking-anywhere-but-at-home-or-on-the-street society, you have probably already caught on to the etiquette if you're a smoker.

Take a few minutes to exchange pleasantries and establish rapport at the start of the visit. Look around and notice any signs of hobbies or special interests that might help you start the conversation. After a few minutes, however, out of respect for time restraints, move on to the objective of your meeting.

If you're having a lunch meeting, don't order alcoholic beverages and choose modestly priced food that's easy to eat—save the lobsters or linguini for social outings. Always wait until the other person is served before beginning to eat.

During an office meeting it's usually fine to take notes, but ask if it's OK first. *Never* run a tape recorder or the other person will feel as if the meeting is an inquisition and clam up. Worse yet, he or she might suspect you are an undeclared reporter.

Frequently restate what you hear the person telling you to reinforce your memory and test your understanding: "In other words, you feel..." or "I understand now that you..." You may consult your list of questions occasionally to keep yourself on track, but don't follow it by rote. Allow the other person to freely develop a line of thinking.

More About Asking Good Questions

W e've all had the experience of being in a meeting with someone we didn't know very well and feeling stuck in an awkward silence. Having a good repertory of questions will get you over any such moments. As we've said before, the first step to comfortable, rapport-building meetings is to have done your background reading. Also, begin your survey by meeting with third-party people first (see page 102). You will build up your confidence with them, and if you don't handle these meetings just as you'd like, it's reassuring to know that they aren't usually as important to your future as other surveying meetings. Both your reading and your initial meetings will stimulate even more sophisticated and potentially revealing questions, which you can incorporate in your later interviews.

Elizabeth, for instance, discovered that, with the exception of the children's fairy tales and pure art books, there seemed to be no history or fiction books based in the medieval period and illustrated as she envisioned. Thus, some of her questions revolved around the economic practicality of doing this. She asked bookstore managers:

■ "To what extent are your customers willing to spend the extra money to buy a beautifully illustrated book?"

■ "How quickly do expensively illustrated fictional or historical books move off your shelves?" (A different way of asking the same question, which provides a double check.)

■ "How much do you feel people will spend for a special children's book as opposed to one for an adult?"

While the bookstore managers felt the retail market might be limited for expensive illustrated books, they felt there was a good market in general and museum libraries. This led Elizabeth to survey the people who purchased for these institutions. She asked the head librarians:

■ "What do you look for in the kind of books I'm describing?"

■ "How are you made aware of the demand for them?"

■ "What sort of interest are you noticing in the medieval period?"

By the time Elizabeth got to the book editors specializing in the type of book she imagined, she was able to provide them with quite a lot of data about current interest in medieval topics and consumer spending habits. Among the questions she asked the editors were:

■ "How would such data as I have gathered influence your acquisitions decisions?"

■ "How important do you feel the library/institutional market is to you as contrasted with retail?"

■ "What type of book would you like to be known for publishing?"

And, because her third-party sources had raised the issue:

■ "How do you feel the advent of the CD-ROM will affect book sales? Do you have plans to tie in your books to interactive software?"

As you become increasingly knowledgeable about the field you are surveying, many of your original questions will be replaced by ones that are aimed toward aspects of the field you may not even have been aware of before. Discussing and role-playing your survey will help you to develop the most useful questions. Seek out the brightest and best-informed friends you have to assist you. After you role-play the meeting with them, ask them to help you brainstorm potential questions.

Try, in each of your survey meetings, to concentrate on questions related to that person's expertise and responsibilities, and ask about

NEED CLUES?

- In your meetings with people, ask what they perceive to be the most important skills to have in the business.
- If it feels appropriate, ask the people you meet if they enjoy working for the organizations they are employed by.
- Read through Chapter 15, in which you are asked to rank

potential employers as to how they meet criteria that stem from the work you've done in earlier chapters. This will help you know what kind of information you should try to pick up in your survey meetings.

- Always be alert to the needs felt by the people and organizations you are visiting.

SURVEYING FOR SALARY INFORMATION

Later on, when you are negotiating the terms of your employment, it will be helpful to know what the average salary is for your people at your level, in your line of work. A good time to find this out is during surveying. Although any discussion of money with people you don't know well can be awkward, you may find that in some meetings you develop a connection that enables you to bring the subject up. It's usually easier with people whom you're pretty sure you will not approach later for work. You'll know if and when it's OK to bring it up. And if you never feel comfortable asking, don't worry. There are other ways to find out about average compensation (see page 158 in Chapter 17).

trends, needs, opportunities, and priorities. Information on these aspects of your interest will determine what you will eventually propose.

Remember to show your enthusiasm, and watch how the other person reacts to it. If you are establishing rapport, you'll know it; if you're not, see if you can find a way to ask how your interviewee feels about some accomplishment. For example, "Closing the Petrie deal seems a remarkable achievement to me. How did you manage to cope with the time pressures and still perform the due diligence required?" A question like that will usually get the conversation going.

One caveat: This is not the time to display your own achievements. (You can do that when you get to proposal meetings, which we'll discuss in Chapter 16.) For the sake of establishing rapport, you can say something like "I know what you mean, I had the same sort of experience when . . ." but then move on. If you try to dazzle someone with your mastery of a subject, you are likely to sound phony or intimidating.

Be sure to end every survey meeting while the other person is still enjoying the conversation. It's always better to leave a little too soon than a little too late, unless your host insists you stay.

"Thank You"

Whenever people spend time with you, in person or on the phone, they deserve a written "thank you." Here are a few rules of thumb that will help ensure that you write effective letters.

Begin by expressing appreciation for their time. Your central paragraph(s) should deal with the substance of your conversation. And, your closing paragraph should include some follow-up action, and repeat your thanks in slightly different words.

In addition to showing your appreciation, your thank-you letter will establish the basis for a return visit, should you choose to have one. The people you interviewed will not forget your courtesy. In most business situations, your letter will be placed in a file and, if you decide to recontact, the letter may be retrieved, reminding these people of your specific interest as well as the care you took to follow up with thanks. Following is a sample thank-you note.

JESSICA BARRETT
293 OVERLOOK COURT
ST. LOUIS, MO 63103

May 18, 1995

Ms. Susan Thomas
Director
Norton-Wallace Associates
2844 Lockwood Boulevard
St. Louis, Missouri 63130

Dear Ms. Thomas,

It was a pleasure meeting with you last Friday. Your powers of concentration in the midst of all the activity you were overseeing were amazing and very much appreciated. The information you gave me about recent events at Norton-Wallace was especially enlightening.

I am particularly intrigued by your insights into what is going on in Sydney. As a direct result of your referral, I had a very productive phone conversation with Ron Sey. As it turned out, he worked on location with East-West Productions in Australia last year with a friend of mine. I might want to be a part of a crew like his, and work my way to Australia. If I do, I'll be sure to let you know, and maybe I can volunteer for the Rainbow Project.

Thank you very much for sharing your enthusiasm and knowledge with me.

Best wishes,

Jessica Barrett

Jessica Barrett

Evaluating What You Have Learned

When you believe your surveying is complete, you will take one of the most important steps in this process: evaluating the information you have gathered.

First go back and read over your survey plan, including the specific topic, the lists of people you intended to see, and the questions you intended to ask. Then read all of your notes from your various meetings, highlighting the most relevant information. At the end of this review, answer these two questions:

- Did you get answers to your questions?

- Did you meet your survey objective?

If you don't feel that you reached your survey objective, you can correct the situation by identifying where valuable information may have slipped through the cracks, and then schedule meetings with a few more people. Before you do, though, consider what happened with respect to your planning, as well as in the meetings you had.

The survey plan:

- Did you develop a clear plan and stick to it?

- Did you actually visit all the people and places you discovered through your background research?

- Did you adhere to the time frame and see at least the number of people mentioned in your objective?

The meetings:

- Were you fully prepared for each meeting?

- Did you keep the conversation focused on your specific topic?

- Did you develop rapport that led to more contacts?

- Did you listen (or were you concentrating on what to say next)?

- Did you ask the questions you had outlined?

- Did you feel nervous?

- Was the time restriction established for the meetings too tight?

If you identify any of these problems, correct them in future meetings and continue to survey until you feel you have fulfilled your objective. On the other hand, you have met your survey objective if you:

■ Had a clear survey plan that you were able to follow.

■ Did your homework before going out on meetings.

■ Prepared relevant and probing questions.

■ Had the number and type of meetings you anticipated.

■ Uncovered information pertinent to your subject.

■ Felt the rapport was good in your meetings.

■ Received appropriate referrals that you later followed up.

■ Kept good records.

■ Still feel enthusiastic about this subject or another related subject to which the survey has led you.

■ Most important, identified sound potential employers (or partners or clients, as the case may be).

To Sum Up

By establishing and carrying out a good survey, you have polished many important research skills. These are skills that professionals and business people value highly. They are the foundation of sound decision-making. You are very near the point when you will see the results of the work you have carried out with this book.

Deciding Where You Want to Work

ALL OF US want to feel good about the decisions we make in life, whether they be about school, work, partnerships, or anything else. But the truth is, most people simply cross their fingers and hope that they make the right choices, especially when it comes to the world of work. Compounding our problems, most of us fail to anticipate changes in the currents of our careers—a boss who moves on, a merger, new technology—and allow the current to carry us where it will rather than following our own course. We may simply not recognize the decisive moment, or if we do recognize it, we don't know how to make a confident decision.

COMING UP

An accurate measuring stick for your next job.

☞ Learn how to match your work to your desires.

☞ Determine and list the specific items that are most important for you to have in your next job.

☞ Prioritize each of these items.

☞ Rank each of your target employers in relation to each of your criteria.

Fortunately, you have already completed most of the work involved in making good decisions. What remains is to extract the key elements from the information you have gathered and decide exactly what's most important to you.

Decision-Making

Decision-making is the process of matching your preferences to the possibilities. By working through this book, you have identified your preferences. These will now be arranged in a criteria list. The organizations you've targeted as possible employers are the possibilities. You will use the same technique to make the match as you might to buy a car. It's ironic that most of us apply more stringent criteria to buying a car than we do to finding a job. Before you headed out to visit car dealers, you probably did a fair amount of thinking and talking about what

> *Good decisions are often made in retrospect when it's too late; they can be made in anticipation.*

you'd like in your next car: reliability, a dealership with a reputation for good service, up-to-date safety devices, attractive lines, high-quality sound system, good acceleration, tight handling, quiet ride, and comfortable, adjustable seats. You probably decided which were the make-or-break items, and you probably also spoke to several other people who had recently purchased new cars. Undoubtedly you made sure that your preferred features were present in the car before you decided to buy.

Well! Follow the same procedure—in a slightly more sophisticated fashion—when you make your next work decision.

What You Know About Yourself and the World

It's time to once again review the work you've done over the course of using this book. Your notebook entries will produce criteria that will go on a decision-making grid or matrix that you'll use to help ensure that you make sound job decisions. It looks like this:

On the long axis of this grid, list all the items that it's important that your next job provide. Work in pencil so it's easy to change your mind. The idea is to include every important factor. Don't worry about the things you think you can't realistically get. Too many people leave important items off their criteria lists because they make assumptions

DECISION-MAKING GRID

CRITERIA	OPTIMAL WEIGHT	TARGET	TARGET	TARGET	TARGET	TARGET	TARGET
PERFECT TOTAL							

that they're too difficult to get. Thinking "I'd never get that," or "That's impossible, I might as well rule that out" simply kills your chances. If it's important to you, put it on your list. You'll be surprised to discover how many of the items on your list will actually be available in your new job. People will be asking you, "How did you ever manage to get such a wonderful situation?"

Start by returning to your plan of action and drawing from the area where you have listed your skill clusters in order of enjoyment and competence. It's important to use at least the top five on your next job, so put them on the list. If you want to list more than five, go ahead, but restrict yourself to the functions you would most enjoy and which you can perform the best.

Next, locate your lists of likes and dislikes. Beginning with people, review the characteristics you absolutely need and those you totally reject. Decide which needs go on the grid, and list them in positive terms.

The number of items you place on the grid is immaterial, but restrict yourself to those that you know will be important in your next work situation. (Don't worry about order. Once you have all items identified, you will take care of ranking them appropriately.)

Go on to your list of likes and dislikes regarding work environment

"On second thought, I don't want the responsibility."

and add those needs to the list in a positive way: "windows that open," "salary of at least $____," and "frequent international travel," or whatever appeals to you. Handle your likes and dislikes regarding community in a similar manner.

The most important items for your grid will come from your goals. Return to your goals statement and reread your back-up notes. Break out the most important elements affecting and affected by your work and translate them, if necessary, into language that will relate to your job decision. For instance, "contributing to alleviating world hunger" might translate into "freedom to develop new long-shelf-life foods for the export line." Or "spending unstressed time daily with my loved ones" might show up on the grid as "requiring less than a 30-minute daily commute."

Focus on each aspect of your goals statement and then ask yourself what qualities a job would need to have to allow this to happen. Typical items that might be added: tuition paid for further study, additional training provided, performance-related compensation, and relocation allowance.

Finally, review your notes on your interests and fascinations to make sure they are represented in your criteria. Likewise, assess your evaluation of your survey and check to be sure that your criteria take into account the important things you've learned.

Take a look at David's first pass at a decision-making grid to get a clearer idea of what all this involves.

When you think you have all of your items identified, reread your criteria list. Is everything important to you on it? You might want to discuss the criteria with your family, bearing in mind that you are always the best judge of what matters to you.

Everything Is Relative

As your criteria list grows longer, you may worry that it's so long that you'll never manage to assess all of the factors. Not to worry; this is why we give each item a ranking. Ask yourself, on a scale of 1 to 20, how important each item is to you? Items that are most important would receive a value of 20. On the other hand, an item that is less important, but still important enough to stay on your list, might

SOME ITEMS ON DAVID'S DECISION-MAKING GRID

CRITERIA	OPTIMAL WEIGHT	TARGET	TARGET	TARGET	TARGET	TARGET	TARGET
A sense that my top skills will be challenged and stretched							
Major proportion of responsibility is presenting to groups							
Availability of sophisticated clients							
In or nearby mountain wilderness							
Opportunity to travel internationally							
Enterprise with clear-cut goals relating to human or community betterment							
$70K minimum annual income with chance to increase by performance							
Small organization in which I can have influence							
Collegial, intelligent associates							
Able to work out of home if I wish							
High degree of autonomy							
Sufficient growth capital available							
One-on-one client consultations							
PERFECT TOTAL							

have a value of 8. (Later, when it comes time to consider a particular job, you will score how close the potential employer comes to meeting the value you have placed on each item.)

Work through your list and assign a numerical value to each criterion. Take your time. Evaluate your criteria in relation to each other until you feel comfortable with the final weight given each of them. (Now you know why you're working in pencil!) In the left column on your grid, write the final number (weight) you have given to each item.

Matching Your Criteria to Your Choices

As a result of your surveying, you have most likely identified several interesting places to work. Across the top of the grid, write in the employers you are considering. (Take a look at the example of David's filled-in grid on page 140. Even though David was primarily thinking of working for himself, he wanted to consider alternatives too, so he could make an informed decision.) If you are still in the survey process, you can add new targets as you identify them. It helps to start ranking your targets while you are in the final survey stage, remembering that the point of surveying is to be able to evaluate your targets before getting into job discussions. You can change your assessments of potential employers several times, but this ranking process makes you very alert as to how things are stacking up as you continue to survey. You may not know the exact ranking for every issue before job discussions begin, but you will have enough information to make strong decisions, if need be.

When you have gathered all the information you need from surveying and you are ready to make proposals, try to finalize your rankings for each of your targets. Carefully review each potential employer relative to each of your criteria.

Take your time. Moving down the column of your criteria, assign a number indicating how close each of your target employers comes to meeting the top weight assigned. Continue until all of your items and targets have been rated.

Add up the totals of each column. Your number-one choice is the one that comes closest to your perfect target total. It's the totals that now guide your decision.

DAVID'S RANKED CRITERIA

CRITERIA	OPTIMAL WEIGHT	TARGET	TARGET	TARGET	TARGET	TARGET	TARGET
A sense that my top skills will be challenged and stretched	20						
Major proportion of responsibility is presenting to groups	15						
Availability of sophisticated clients	18						
In or nearby mountain wilderness	18						
Opportunity to travel internationally	10						
Enterprise with clear-cut goals relating to human or community betterment	20						
$70K minimum annual income with chance to increase by performance	15						
Small organization in which I can have influence	12						
Collegial, intelligent associates	16						
Able to work out of home if I wish	14						
High degree of autonomy	20						
Sufficient growth capital available	15						
One-on-one client consultations	19						
PERFECT TOTAL	212						

Going Into Business for Yourself

Even if you're planning to freelance, do consulting work, or start your own business, use a decision-making grid and compare your choice to employment alternatives. It's important to submit your undertaking to the same rigorous analysis that you would any other venture, since it's your own time and capital that are at risk.

The extraordinarily high failure rate for small businesses stems in large measure from the failure to do such an analysis. The principals find themselves disappointed or unable to make a profit and the ventures go down the drain. Being an independent contractor or starting your own business may be the perfect answer for you, but you need to test it and make sure it measures up. David was quite amazed to discover that independent consulting did not rate the highest on his decision-making grid. This was primarily because he didn't think he'd be able to get the high-level clients and colleagues that more established firms would be able to deliver, and because he would be in a riskier financial situation.

DAVID'S EMPLOYMENT TARGETS RANKED

CRITERIA	OPTIMAL WEIGHT	CONNOR CORP.	LORAN ASSOC.	INDEPENDENT CONSULTING	WYATT LEARNING SYSTEMS	CREATIVE LEARNING INC.	HUGHES TRAINING	INTER-TRAIN
A sense that my top skills will be challenged and stretched	20	17	14	15	18	20	8	12
Major proportion of responsibility is presenting to groups	15	12	10	7	15	15	15	15
Availability of sophisticated clients	18	16	16	14	13	18	7	11
In or nearby mountain wilderness	18	16	14	16	10	18	16	16
Opportunity to travel internationally	10	0	10	5	10	7	8	10
Enterprise with clear-cut goals relating to human or community betterment	20	12	12	20	12	20	5	10
$70K minimum annual income with chance to increase by performance	15	14	13	10	12	10	12	15
Small organization in which I can have influence	12	10	10	12	6	12	0	4
Collegial, intelligent associates	16	14	14	0	11	16	10	10
Able to work out of home if I wish	14	2	2	14	8	10	0	2
High degree of autonomy	20	7	7	20	13	18	3	5
Sufficient growth capital available	15	15	10	8	15	10	15	12
One-on-one client consultations	19	19	19	19	0	19	10	10
PERFECT TOTAL	212	154	151	160	143	109	193	132

You may choose to work independently even if that option does not win your top total on your decision-making grid. But if you've done your surveying and compared it to other options, you'll be doing so with a greater awareness of where the pitfalls lie. Armed with this knowledge, you can seek partners or employees who can supply what you cannot.

There are many good references available in bookstores and libraries that will help you make a sound business plan if you decide to go out on your own. The caution we express here is meant to assure your careful initial decision.

To Sum Up

Criteria ranking helps you take all of your information—even such highly subjective information as feelings—and put it in a measurable form. If you follow the method carefully, it is relatively simple and straightforward. When you have worked through your criteria and assigned a value to each, you will know which employers to approach first. Afterward, when you are evaluating them, referring to your decision-making grid will enable you to avoid the muddled thinking that almost always develops when you try to compare one target with another; targets should always be evaluated against your criteria, not against each other.

When you have finished surveying, establishing criteria, and rating your targets, you are ready to make the pitch for that new job. In the eyes of the people who will be considering you, you'll be far ahead of other candidates because you know more about yourself and about them than the vast majority of people they would consider hiring.

From Surveys to Proposals

THERE'S NO SUBSTITUTE for self-confidence and no better time to feel confident than when you're looking for a new job. When Elizabeth realized that she was getting close to putting her interest in medieval art and writing to work, she felt so confident and energized that her friends commented on her new vitality. Knowing that she was finally getting close to the issues that were important to her, she was even able to fly through her more pedestrian writing and editing assignments. Of course, all this was no happy accident. Elizabeth had carried her survey twice as far as she had planned. Now, after three months, she had identified four publishers whose market orientation and style of art reproduction matched her own standards.

COMING UP

The secrets of:
☛ Preparing a successful proposal for each of your top targets.
☛ Being in peak form when presenting your proposals.
☛ Feeling reassured that the work you want is within your reach.

Elizabeth had grasped what all surveyors must learn: You survey to reveal targets—and their perceived needs. She felt equal to meeting these needs, and she was now ready to propose her services—actually, to propose a job.

The route Elizabeth traveled to get to this point involved several steps in sequence:

1. Discovering her best skills

2. Marrying those skills to her foremost interests

3. Developing a concept of what she would like to accomplish

4. Surveying her concept until she could identify both targets and their needs

5. And, finally, proposing a job

Making Proposals

Picture this: The people you want to hire you are listening attentively as you enthusiastically and confidently describe how you will help them meet their needs. This is the moment you've been preparing for. Because you have done your homework, it's easier than you might expect. You have thoroughly analyzed your skills and interests, marshaled your experience, and surveyed the field. Most important, you've researched the organization and determined that you can meet some of its needs. During surveying you will have likely picked up a sense of how the people you met with might like to be approached—and you use this to your advantage, tailoring your approach to their style. All of this will help you make your proposal hit the mark.

FREELANCERS TAKE NOTE

Even if you're considering going into business for yourself, as David was, you owe yourself a proposal just as much—logically even more—as potential employers. A proposal of what you will do for yourself will help you focus your thoughts and get ready to make a business plan. So don't skip over this chapter if you are in David's shoes.

Effective Proposals

Whether you're going for a staff position or a consultancy, presenting a fabulous proposal—that is, describing clearly what you can do for the organization—is the key to getting the job you want. Many people applying for staff positions believe that all they need to show is their past experience and respond to interview questions, not realizing that proposals may be crucial to their success. Proposals indicate that you are interested enough to go beyond standard expectations. They may be particularly important if the job you want is different from the jobs you've held in the past. Employers need to be able to feel reassured that their present needs will be met. The purpose of a proposal is to demonstrate to them that they will.

Proposals are usually presented orally first and then later in writing. Even if you only plan to deliver your proposal orally, always write it out first. Working on paper forces you to clarify your thinking and helps ensure that you include all your points. Also, at the end of a proposal meeting, you may be asked to leave behind a copy of your proposal so that others can consider it.

You will ensure your success by:

■ Developing a compelling opening statement that captures the purpose of your proposal—*why I am here.*

■ Defining the needs (discovered in surveying) you can address for the organization—*what is needed.*

■ Outlining how can you meet these needs—*what I will do for you.*

■ Supporting each point you make with convincing evidence (drawn from your knowledge of yourself)—*why it will work.*

■ Determining one or more action steps the decision-maker and you can take in order to come to agreement—*how to take the next step.*

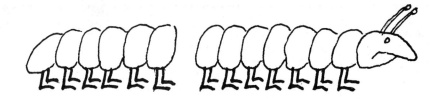

S. GROSS

"I've decided to start my own caterpillar."

Why I Am Here

Your opening statement must capture the essence of what you intend to do for the decision-maker. Stirring examples of opening statements include President John F. Kennedy's ". . . to put a man on the moon and return him safely to earth within the decade," and Mark Anthony's "I come to bury Caesar, not to praise him." Granted, your proposal may not be as grandiose. You might wish to show a software company ". . . the effectiveness of standardizing 'help' responses" or demonstrate how a toy manufacturer can "assemble and package board games more efficiently," or how an arts organization can ". . . attract new audiences by initiating family performances."

Elizabeth captured publishers' attention by suggesting she could help them increase market interest and demand for beautifully illustrated books by helping to produce attractive historical publications that would appeal to educational institutions as well as the retail buyer.

Taking your number-one target first, review all of the information that you've accumulated about it, and construct the opening statement to your proposal.

Refine your opening statement and try it out on friends. Ask if they know *immediately* what you are talking about and if you have created a sense of anticipation. Keep polishing the statement until you feel certain that you have an attention-getter.

Your opening statement is followed by a clear statement of "what is needed."

NEED CLUES?

- Start by outlining the principal points of your proposal, underlining the key words, and gradually forming a brief sentence to introduce the essence of what you can do for them.

- Look at it from the decision-maker's point of view: Do you remember any concepts or words he or she expressed in a previous meeting? How are these important to your opening statement? Can you incorporate them?

- Make the statement vivid by using an appealing image or idea: "extend and secure your market," "cut complaints in half," "produce an event that will make the evening news," "prepare the company to be a contender for the Malcolm Baldrige Award."

What Is Needed

People hire you for one main reason: You can address one or more of their perceived needs. *The decision-maker must be convinced that hiring you offers benefits greater than the cost of bringing you on board.* Many job seekers miss this obvious point.

Think of their need as a gap between where the person is now and where she or he wants to be. The size of the gap reflects the size of the need. The job you are proposing will fill the gap for the employer. For example, if you were preparing a proposal for a mountain resort, you might be able to:

- Improve room service
- Cut down waiting time at registration
- Increase the number of day skiers and overnight guests

For an electrical parts distributor, you might be able to:

- Reduce back orders
- Eliminate lost or misplaced orders
- Reorganize assembly and shipping
- Slow, stop, or reverse increasing personnel costs

One caveat: If you see a gap but the employer isn't concerned about it or doesn't admit that it exists, then save yourself the trouble of even making a proposal. Potential employers will take a long time to be moved to answer needs that they do not perceive. If you have placed such an employer among your top targets, you can expect a very long and probably unsuccessful time trying to convince the person you are right. Surveying will usually keep you from getting into such predicaments, because you wouldn't be writing a proposal if your survey meetings had not already revealed needs that employers are likely to want filled.

> *Jobs are needs perceived by the employer. It's as simple as that.*

If you discover at this point that you don't know enough to speak to the employer's needs, return to surveying until you have a better understanding. At this point surveying that focuses on the needs of others relative to your concept, rather than on your own needs, produces the information you require.

Need Clues?

- Can you identify an essential quality the product or service is lacking?
- What does this organization need to do to maintain current business in its competitive environment?
- What new market might you help them capture?
- What problem did your survey source mention in your meeting(s)? What was missing in the organization? What opportunities were going begging?
- Put yourself in the place of the person to whom you are presenting. What would you like to hear? What *must* you hear to make a decision?
- What do organizations in this field typically need that corresponds to what you want to do?
- Consider the following "need" categories:
  - Savings on expenses
  - Increasing revenues and profit margins
  - Exploiting new markets for products or services
  - Reorganizing for productivity
  - Improving how people work together
  - Improving customer service
  - Upgrading quality

What I Will Do for You

Once you have stated the problem you intend to address, it is time to offer your solution. You must be very specific so the person listening gets a clear picture of the possibilities. You will want to include:

- What you will do personally and/or as part of a team

- Who should be involved

- The tools you will need to deliver the results

A complex proposal is not always better; the ones that succeed are often quite simple. Give enough details to show that you know what you're talking about, but not enough information so that the task could be accomplished without you. In your preparatory work you will have thought of many details that do not have to be put forward until you have been already hired.

Remember to look at the problem through the decision-maker's eyes. For each step of the solution you propose, mention a direct benefit to the person or company. "Benefits" describe what the other person or the organization will receive that is valued. They may be expressed as increased earnings, lower overhead, relief from unpleasant tasks or worry, more customers, reduced personnel turnover, or improved staff attitude, among many other things.

If your solution is complex, present only the main steps and benefits. It's usually the benefit that the decision-maker feels personally that will seal the deal. For example, if a recommended step is to "Organize a letter-writing campaign to potential underwriters to increase revenue for your annual charity auction," you might add "My preliminary survey of the market tells me we could expect an increase of at least 25 percent in responses and monies taken in. I know it would be a relief to you to know that your basic costs are taken care of before the event ever occurs."

Try to anticipate the decision-maker's concerns or objections to your suggestions and include your responses to these in your presentation. Usually when someone objects, he is asking to be convinced.

For example, if you anticipate the objection, "We don't have enough time to get together a list of potential underwriters," you might say "Being aware of the heavy work load of your present staff, I have already assembled a list of the most probable potential underwriters." (*But don't give away the list until you're hired.*)

Notice how these job seekers coupled their solutions with projected benefits to the company:

> "I can organize and do all of the ordering needed to rent equipment for your booth at the convention and, because of a software program I recently installed on my computer, I believe I can accomplish this in very little time."

> "After I conduct a productivity study, I can write a report giving a picture of where you are now. You will then be able to select from several recommendations, with time, cost, and personnel savings for each included."

> "I envision a payback period of four months for the automated order and record-keeping I propose. Personnel costs should level off in about six months and decline in one year, unless, of course, we experience a significant rise in business, in which case the payback will be much sooner."

Why It Will Work

Up to this point your proposal may make good sense to anyone who hears it. But to convince your top choice to give you a green light, you must provide evidence that you personally can make it succeed.

In your notebook or computer, consult your "Talking Papers." Find examples of times when you used the exact skills needed to carry out this proposal. Here is where you tell the decision-maker that what you will be doing comes naturally to you and that you have done similar things with good results before. Choose examples that will appeal to this particular individual. Here's what some other people have said.

> "I worked for six years in my father's sign shop processing silk-screened signs by the hundreds. We developed a procedure for handling and shipping with unusual speed. Later, my inventory-control project at Hastings successfully identified typical problem spots in storing, shipping, and order processing, to the point that customer complaints fell to a 2 percent frequency."

> "In the ski shop where I worked in Utah, I used my own computer to record inventory, prices, and correspondence. The owner was so pleased with the improved efficiency, I was promoted to manager after seven months."

> "At J & R Consulting I was assigned the Safe Shop account and succeeded in helping them reduce spoilage by half and decrease purchase expenses on produce by 7 percent."

Don't forget to use other sources to build evidence that supports your proposal. Giving examples of what the competition is doing and quoting outside experts can help you prove your point.

> "My research revealed that the largest distributors are using sophisticated systems and a few now on the market are applicable to an operation your size."

> "This chart I developed shows how your competition within a 100-mile radius is doing with respect to equipment rentals and occupancy rates."

F R O M   S U R V E Y S   T O   P R O P O S A L S

How to Take the Next Step

Close the proposal by making sure that, for all the trouble and time you have invested, *something will happen.*

Begin your conclusion by summarizing your main points; mention the top one or two things you would accomplish. Then add their benefits. Keep the summary brief so that your listener(s) can remember it after you have left. Finally, ask the decision-maker to take an appropriate action. This action might be one of three types:

■ Something the decision-maker can do while you are there.

■ Something the decision-maker can do after you have left.

■ A request that you provide additional information to facilitate further discussion and decision-making.

Be sensitive to constraints under which the other person may be operating (a special event, vacation, or product launch coming up, a pressing problem that needs immediate attention) and remember that he or she might have to consult others before making a final decision. Here are some examples of closings:

> "Perhaps we could speak again after you have had a chance to review my estimates with your comptroller."

> "What would you say to our getting together next Wednesday to further discuss this?"

> "If you agree, perhaps you could look over this chart which indicates where new business may come from. I think you'll see why I'm so excited about the prospects. I'd like to make my move before the new season gets underway, so perhaps we could talk in the next few days."

Further Pointers

Review your proposal carefully for any omissions and practice delivering it to a friend. Just how irresistible can you be in 15 minutes or less?

Make sure you have you covered all five points: 1) Why I am here. 2) What is needed. 3) What I will do. 4) Why it will work. 5) How to take the next step.

In addition, make sure that the main points are supported by clearly outlined benefits to the decision-maker or the organization, and ask your-

151

self if your evidence is convincing. Remember that in addition to citing examples from your talking papers, you may quote outside experts, statistics, survey observations, trends, competitors' experience, and your own knowledge about the subject.

Each target requires a unique proposal devised with that particular decision-maker and organization in mind. In most cases you will make the proposal in person, but be prepared to either leave a written proposal behind, or deliver it within a day or two of your oral presentation if you wish to make changes based on the meeting. You may want to polish it a little or add some nugget of additional information that augments a point made during your presentation.

Remember,
people, not
pieces of paper,
open doors.
—John C. Crystal

If you choose to include charts, pictures and graphs, make sure they look great. Graphics can be enormously effective, but if they are not prepared professionally, it's better to do without them. In this media-sensitive world, when you're providing images, make them impressive or do not provide them at all. The best image you can put forth is yourself: smiling, confident, comfortable in your clothes, and on target with what you are proposing.

Present proposals to all of your targets in rapid succession—all in the same week, if possible. You want each of your decision-makers moving to take action at the same time, which positions you to make the best possible deal. In all likelihood you will be proposing to people you met during your survey, which means that securing appointments will be relatively easy. If it turns out that the person you met is not the right person, but your rapport is good (and you should only be making proposals to people with whom you've established a good rapport), he or she will most likely be happy to recommend you to the appropriate decision-maker.

A final point: Avoid getting rushed into a discussion of your compensation until the decision-maker has considered all the other points of your proposal. Negotiations over what to pay you (covered in the next chapter) will go much better if the benefits you bring to the enterprise are already well understood. Simply say "If we decide we have a good match between what I propose and what you need, I am sure we will be able to agree on the compensation involved."

To Sum Up

Design your oral presentation to last no longer than 15 minutes. You want to be brief, to the point, and compelling. Your most important guideline is always to remember the point of view of the person to whom you are presenting. His or her perspective should govern what you present, how you present it, and how you answer questions along the way. If you offer solutions to the decision-maker's view of the problems, you're most likely to find success.

Negotiating the Relationship

Y OUR GOLDEN MOMENT is nearing. You've come to the point that when the proposals you've been making have produced an eagerness to bring you on board, and you need to prepare to negotiate the terms of your relationship. Just as you were proposing to more than one organization, you will likely be negotiating with more than one, because you can't know that it's a sure thing until you have an agreement on the cost and conditions of your employment. The preparation for this stage is often overlooked or avoided by job seekers who feel themselves to be the victim of someone else's system. Your work with this book, how-

COMING UP

A satisfying end point (for now) to all your good work!

☞ Review your decision-making criteria and, if you wish, adjust the order of your targets.

☞ Learn where and when to negotiate.

☞ Rehearse negotiating.

☞ Learn tips on how to make negotiations smooth and profitable.

ever, has prepared you to exercise an appropriate amount of control when you come to this stage. Plus, the information you have at your disposal because of your surveying has prepared you to be realistic in your approach to negotiating. You are an agent on your own behalf—not a passive applicant hoping that you pleased the interviewer.

There is a way to approach negotiating that takes the cold feet and clammy hands often associated with discussions of this sort out of the equation. This chapter will lead you through the steps, help you to visualize and practice your negotiations, and conclude with both you and your employer feeling you got a good deal. A nice thought? Let's make it happen.

Getting Close

You know you are close to the negotiating point when you feel that you have established why you are the best person for the job, and that your potential employer is eager to have you on board. The signals are usually clear: The decision-maker makes references to points you have raised and mentions quoting you to others in the organization; you're having an easy time getting through on the phone or getting another meeting set up; other people are invited to meet with you to discuss what you are proposing; people in the organization talk about what you could accomplish with them; or the decision-maker might

"Hey! How much to water the lawn?"

simply say "Well, when can you start?" Things can move very quickly from proposals into negotiations, so it's wise to get prepared for negotiating when you are in the final stages of presenting your proposals.

A word about additional meetings with others in the organization during the proposal stage: Be very careful to project yourself as a resource and a help to those already in the organization and not a potential threat. The trick is to figure out how to make them look good too. For example, you might say to a future colleague something like:

> "Perhaps when I am on board I can locate the research I did at Zenlon on non-deteriorating fibers. It might help you solve the knitting machine problem you describe."

> "I'll send you the article I ran across the other day. It really backs up the point I hear you making on employee training."

You want other employees in the organization to feel you'd be great to work with. The rapport you generate with those who will be your peers is as important as the relationship you are building with your potential boss.

When to Begin Negotiations

The right time to begin negotiations is when you have established the benefits of having you on board and you have a good feeling about the mutual benefits of such an association.

Never talk money until the very end of your proposal discussions. Your chances of achieving your optimum compensation and working conditions are much greater after the decision-maker has become convinced of your value. If pressed too early in the process, say clearly that you are certain you can arrive at a fair compensation once you are both sure that you are the right person for the job.

As you prepare to enter your negotiations, remember that the best thing going for you is your mutual enthusiasm for the task(s) outlined in your proposal. When two people want to accomplish the same thing, they generally find a way.

Think about how you felt when you decided to buy a car; once you found the model you were crazy about, you couldn't wait to be driving it. Well, maybe you've just managed to make your potential employer feel that way about you.

Before You Negotiate

Go back to the decision-making grid you made in Chapter 15 on which you ranked your criteria for your next job. Review your targets once more in relation to your criteria. Your proposal meetings have probably revealed more about the people you would be working with and you may want to rethink your top choices. Following your review and any adjustments in your ratings, add up your totals again. Has the order of your targets changed? You will want to negotiate with all of your top targets at the same time if you can possibly manage it. Naturally, you will be pressing for your number-one choice. You may be willing to make more trade-offs to land that job, but you won't let them know it.

Determine your salary and compensation range in advance. Through surveying, you may have gotten a sense of what similar jobs pay. If you are still uncertain, you can get quick information from the field's professional associations, trade magazines, employment ads in the newspaper, the *Occupational Outlook Handbook*, and the *National Business Employment Weekly*. Based on your personal needs, you decide:

1. The minimum that you must earn

2. What the organization is likely to pay, given the norms and competition in the industry

3. What you would be *most* happy earning

4. Your likely value to the organization

An employer weighs the compensation he or she will offer you against industry norms, the organization's overall needs, how much revenue you are likely to generate, your previous salary, your education, your experience, and perhaps even your appeal to the competition.

To figure out the likely negotiating range, determine the lowest compensation you would take and estimate the highest amount you think the organization will pay. Your salary will likely fall somewhere in between these two numbers.

Don't be concerned if you are not an experienced negotiator; most of us aren't, but it is a skill that can be learned and will be useful to you throughout life. Once you have read through the whole chapter

NEED CLUES?

- If you need information on salary, your library has material on salary ranges in your field. You can also call a professional association—they have salary information for their fields. In addition, all government offices, utilities, and publicly held corporations publish salary information.

- Think about how much this employer feels your skills are needed and to what extent other employees possess them already.

- How much would this employer worry if you were hired by the competition?

- How understaffed or overstaffed is this employer?

- How comprehensive and convincing is the evidence that you can get the job done?

- Is your proposal in line with the organization's priorities?

- How much do you and your potential employer like each other?

and have your information in line, find a friend and practice until you start to feel comfortable. Hearing yourself say aloud the phrases you will use in negotiating creates the reality. Ask your friend to give you feedback on how you are coming across.

Before the meeting, try to visualize an ideal (but realistic) negotiation. See yourself comfortably seated, enjoying a pleasant, purposeful conversation. Imagine the sequence of negotiation topics and the decision-maker responding in a positive way. Envision the two of you shaking hands at the successful conclusion of your discussion.

The Negotiation Itself

The best negotiations are mutual efforts by two parties to allocate the benefits each has to offer the other in such a way that both profit. In the Crystal-Barkley process, negotiations aim to set fair terms for enlisting commitment and effort. The object of a negotiation is to reach an agreement that works.

The best negotiations are between peers. Fortunately, your surveying and proposal conversations with your targeted employers have brought you to a position where you feel equal to them because they now view you as a desired resource. This is an enormous achievement. If you wonder how you did it, think about what you have already accomplished:

- You have demonstrated your value to the organization.

- You provided proof that you are up to the job.

- You have conveyed your enthusiasm to the decision-maker and he or she is now feeling enthusiastic too.

- You feel sure that this opportunity will meet your own needs.

In fact, in your own minds, you and your targeted employer have each already made a deal; all that's left is to settle the details.

Since all of the trouble you have taken in surveying and presenting proposals has in all likelihood led you to have more than one target, you are in a position to negotiate freely: You know you have other viable possibilities. *A good negotiator always feels it is possible to walk away from the table if basic criteria are not met.* Your alternatives make you free and your skills and knowledge make you equal to the situation.

> *The most satisfactory negotiations are carried on by those who have a sense of being equal to each other.*

Aim to get the employer to put a compensation figure on the table first. Parry as long as you can, and if you cannot elicit the offer, tell the person with whom you are negotiating that you were thinking of a figure "in the neighborhood of," something just slightly above what you believe to be the top of the organization's range. It would be a mistake to start the negotiation at a figure you know to be far above the top of the range, and you might offend the decision-maker if you name a figure higher than he or she makes. This is where your homework will stand you in good stead.

Once a figure is mentioned, whether the decision-maker does it or you do, the negotiation has begun in the true sense. From here on, it is a sophisticated game, with each of you taking turns justifying why your figures make sense. In making your case, be sure to use examples that illustrate why you are worth what you are asking:

> "The 20 percent reduction in customer complaints I conservatively project should save about $90,000 in returns alone, and free up staff to put on the direct marketing effort."

> "I predict these new events will bring in 500 new members, which will translate into over $32,000 in increased revenue."

See how the information you have gathered enables you to create realistic scenarios of what you can do?

Discuss the basic salary or commission figure until you arrive at the number that reflects a sound mutual understanding of expectation. Be careful not to push it so far that the other person becomes uncomfortable or resistant. Careful observation of body language will aid you in this. Only when the basic compensation figure is agreed upon are you in a good position to discuss bonuses, additional compensation possibilities, or working conditions. The order of your discussion is very important. In every important negotiation about a job, the following eight items are on the table (and possibly more). To ensure that the negotiation proceeds positively and in a manner likely to produce the best outcome for you, *always* discuss issues in the following order.

1. Deal with the basic numbers: salary, fee, commission percentage.

2. Introduce the add-on numbers: bonus, or other performance-based compensation.

3. Discuss fringe benefits: health insurance, pension, stock.

4. Identify perks: expense account, clubs, moving expenses.

5. Seek the most favorable working conditions that will allow you to carry out your proposal well: support staff, office location, orientation and training, resources (such as consultants, computer hardware and software, membership in professional associations), flexible schedule, authority and control, working at home, vacation.

6. Ask for continuing education and training: professional conferences, tuition allowances, in-house training, mentoring systems.

7. Determine how your work will be measured: Set the standards and learn the timing of performance appraisals. (It's often possible to negotiate for earlier than normal appraisals, which can speed up raises and promotions.)

8. Explore opportunities for advancement and promotion.

In addition, if there are any other criteria that are important to you, bring them up now. You already know the relative importance of these criteria, so you know which to insist on and which to let go.

The reason order is of such importance in this discussion is that you want to avoid weighing the advantages and costs of items which really aren't comparable. For example, were you to discuss the importance of a training course and agree on this before you have agreed on your salary or fee, you may find that the cost of this course is assumed to be deducted from your pay. Take care to guide the discussion to each item in order: Agree on the dollar figure attached to each, and finalize the discussion on each issue before moving on to the next. Try to cover all of the items of importance to you; after the job starts, you will never have the same opportunity to establish ideal working conditions as you do now.

Always be careful to get your offer in writing after your negotiation is complete. If the decision-maker hesitates, offer to prepare a draft for him or her to review that reflects your understanding. This will spare him or her the trouble of writing one and will enable you to be sure all points are covered. The other person can then put your draft on company letterhead and sign off on it. You may well be asked to sign this document as well.

If you have to quit your present job in order to accept this offer, do not— we repeat, do not—quit until you have a firm, written offer and a starting date. It occasionally happens that events beyond anyone's control make it impossible for a decision-maker to make good on an offer. You can end up out in the cold if you jump too soon.

To Sum Up

You are on your way to making your next work decision; more important, you are on the way to accomplishing your goals in life. If you've been carrying on two or three negotiations at one time—and we sincerely hope this is the case—you may have to decide which are the best deals within a matter of days. Review your requirements and expectations before making your final decision and ask yourself these important questions:

- "What will I accomplish by taking this job?"

- "How will taking this job affect my lifestyle? How will it affect those close to me?"

- "Am I still as comfortable with these people as I initially thought?"

■ "To what future job would this position logically lead me?"

■ "Will I be able to lead my life in a way that I want if I take this job?"

■ "What will be the immediate and long-range personal and professional impacts of this job?"

And finally, ask yourself:

■ "Will I be better off if I take this job than if I stay where I am for the immediate future?"

If you can answer to each of these questions positively, give yourself the green light.

On the other hand, if the answer to these questions make you feel uncomfortable, hold off on making a decision. Perhaps a short period of additional surveying will bring more information to the surface that will eliminate your uncertainties. No one can ever be 100 percent sure of any decision, but your experience surveying and making proposals normally provides ample assurance that you are making the best possible decision.

We can guarantee that your new employer or clients will be getting a lot for their money by hiring you. Besides, they are getting something else that is indispensible in every enterprise: someone who knows how to negotiate effectively. The most savvy employers are aware of this and, on a very deep level, they feel satisfied if you have fairly represented yourself.

Everybody wins when you head off to work on Monday mornings looking forward to the tasks ahead. Congratulations to you and to your employer when you achieve this!

Long-term Survival and Satisfaction

A S YOU CONTEMPLATE your new future, you may be curious to know what happened to our friends Elizabeth and David. Elizabeth's first-choice publisher carried on discussions with her for several weeks but in the end decided not to proceed. Her second choice, with whom discussions had gone on for almost as long, accepted her proposal, but not until she brought in her Yale professor friend as a possible author. His prestige and experience (and the fact that Elizabeth had such easy access to him) proved to be just the credibility factor she needed to tip the scales. The publisher offered her a position as an editor, with the idea that she'd create a new line of books featuring medieval history and illustrations as well as take on responsibility for other projects. In retrospect she was grateful she had been so avid about surveying and that she'd maintained contact with the professor as well as with several other people.

COMING UP

A foundation for a successful, happy work life—now and in the future.

☞ Learn to look ahead and to anticipate the hurdles that you may face.

☞ Discover ways to work that help you do your best.

☞ Read about ways to help keep your goals fresh and meaningful.

David had a longer route to travel than Elizabeth, due mainly to his feelings about what his information had shown. It took him a while to adjust to the fact that independent consulting had turned up *second* in his criteria rating. During his surveying he had thought he would really like to be on his own. However, his criteria rating convinced him to rethink his situation. One of the companies he'd surveyed, Creative Learning, was a very attractive option. It ran out of a ranch in Nevada; the principal and majority owner was a man who had built his reputation around leading seminars on business renewal and reorganization. He offered most of his training to groups at the ranch and the rest at various corporate retreats around the world. Since the principal was getting along in years, David decided to propose a gradual buy-out, to be financed in part by his own work—sweat equity, so to speak.

> *Serendipity is the fortunate coincidence of luck and awareness.*

It turned out that he approached the owner at a fortuitous time. The owner's wife had been trying to persuade him to plan for the future. This was an instance of serendipity about which we often hear our surveying and proposing clients talk.

The principal of Creative Learning and David agreed that David would start work as a contractor for a fee until they both felt he was completely proficient in delivering the training. At that point David would move into a salaried position, managing and marketing as well as giving seminars.

Both David and Elizabeth were elated over the results of their hard work. It had taken a while, but so much less time than a bad or dissatisfying decision would have cost them. They knew they had much hard work before them too. So they were dumbfounded when we told them that, strange as it may seem, the time to start planning for your next job is when you get a new one.

"Wait a minute," they said, "What's going on? Let us enjoy the fruits of our efforts. It was hard work getting to this point."

We don't intend to rob you of the pleasure of having "arrived," but we do want to make the job search easier for you the next time around, and the next, and the next. You have already built the foundation, and your plan of action, even now, suggests the future steps in work and non-work that you envision taking. By all means, enjoy the gratification of having found this interesting job, but recognize that it is one step of many. Make your future steps easier by planning for them on a continual basis.

The last item another client, Alice, talked about with the manufacturer hiring her as vice president for training and development was her future career path. The manufacturer wasn't put off by her raising the issue; on the contrary, he was encouraged that Alice did not see herself staying in her new position forever. Employers are looking for an appropriate amount of ambition in their new hires—*appropriate* being the key word. Talking about immediate promotions is out of order during negotiations for a new job. But conveying the part of your long-range goals that coincides with the corporate mission is a nice way of saying you have come on the team for more than the dollars involved.

How to Look Ahead

That feeling of peaks and valleys—"Everything's cool" versus "My life's a mess"—disappears as you absorb the principles of the Crystal-Barkley process into your life. Your progress now takes on a different character, with you in control and on a steadier course, knowing that when disappointments come, they are but temporary difficulties along your path.

When Sandy first came to Crystal-Barkley, he felt like disaster was impending. He was one of several lawyers for a large multinational corporation that was busily acquiring other companies. Sandy had become increasingly disturbed by the actions of one of the senior corporate officers with whom he worked on closing deals. He felt this executive was purposely withholding pertinent information in order to gain unfair advantage in some of the deals; the practice was not only unethical but in the end could be damaging to the parent company. Although Sandy knew he should bring it up, he also knew the executive had the power to damage his future with the company. Sandy was in a classic catch-22. He thought the only way out was to resign.

An examination of Sandy's skills and goals led us to conclude that aside from the problem with his colleague, the prospects for his future with the company were bright. After Sandy did a survey and lined up some alternatives outside his company, he decided to risk expressing his concerns to the CEO. At the same time, he made a sideline proposal to provide some company-wide ethics-in-negotiating seminars, as well as to do some monitoring that would discourage questionable negotiating in the future. Prominent in Sandy's skills sets was a strong capacity to deliver convincing and appealing presentations. Another great aspect of Sandy's proposing to lead the seminars was that he would have to move near the corporate headquarters—located near an area where he and his wife wanted to move.

Sandy's proposal to the CEO was accepted with few modifications. The problem executive eventually left the corporation, perhaps finding his activities too closely scrutinized. Sandy worked his way up in the counsel's office, hoping to eventually run one of the company's acquisitions. When corporate politics prevented that move, he chose to take early retirement and pursue another of his primary interests—one he had thoroughly surveyed. Sandy now raises an exotic breed of thoroughbred horses and has turned it into a profitable business.

All of this activity took place over more than 10 years. The point is that Sandy had an overall game plan, with alternatives built in, which he kept refining as new information surfaced from ongoing surveys. He measured how long to stay in each new situation by the levels of *enjoyment he derived and the effectiveness he was able to display.* If his path appeared blocked in one direction, he sometimes persisted and sometimes sidestepped to a more amenable route that fit his talents and the needs at hand. Continuing surveying produced alternatives and gave him a sense of freedom and control. Everything didn't always work out exactly as he foresaw, but were you to ask Sandy today, he would tell you that he is happier with his life than he dreamed possible.

Overall, you can steer your future course by:

■ Continuing to explore your interests.

■ Evaluating which of your interests are most appropriate to your work-for-pay activity.

■ Taking the initiative in presenting proposals to your current employer, as well as to future ones or to clients, partners, or financiers.

■ Accommodating your interests that seem purely avocational by engaging in recreational activities, travel, learning experiences, and volunteering.

Do Your Best

In your new job your primary concern is to confirm the good judgment of the person who hired you, whether you're on staff or working as an independent. Try to *exceed* expectations. You can do it this way:

1. Set up the best possible office systems.

2. Observe carefully the behavior of and relationships between your peers and superiors.

3. Express quiet enthusiasm, and withhold excessive comment.

4. Survey for the best resources, both inside and outside of the organization, to help you do your job.

5. Deliver superb work in a timely manner.

Set up the best possible office systems. Nothing beats being organized, and the best time to do it is at the beginning of a job or an assignment. If you wait, the crush of accumulating details will consume your time, and you will be run ragged trying to put your hands on the right piece of information at the right time. You may also make a poor showing if you are unable to produce answers when they are needed.

Arrange your office space so that the tools you use most often are closest to you. Be sure you have a comfortable chair and desk, even if you have to buy them yourself! Check your lighting and add an incandescent lamp, if needed. Plan to input most of your information into a computer, keeping regular backup disks to avoid loss, and set up files for hard copies of critical information: agreements, contracts, illustrations, all incoming correspondence, summary memos, and the like. You may have an assistant who can manage much of this for you, but you should absolutely know how to retrieve information yourself, because at critical moments, your assistant might not be there. Discipline yourself to file information as soon as it is acted upon. For more information on getting organized, see Appendix A, page 177.

Observe carefully the behavior and the relationships of your peers and superiors. Take every opportunity to attend meetings, accept casual lunch or coffee invitations, and study the work of others. By observing and listening carefully to conversations and the answers to your occasional questions, you learn how things are being done and also begin to form a refined sense of the political structure of your department and the organization overall. You will discover that it is not always the official decision-maker who makes the decisions. You will learn the quirks and foibles of your colleagues and bosses and adjust your own behavior if it is in your best interests. You will catch on to how other people best assimilate the information you give them (in writing, orally, first thing in the morning, over a beer after work...). You will learn their blatant and hidden agendas.

All of this information gives you the power you need to make the impact you wish to make in this job. Remember, your plan is to be the "value added," not to duplicate the work of others. You want to pick up where they leave off, helping to facilitate what they're already doing, and studying how you can most quickly deliver the benefits the person who hired you expects. Be part of the team. This advice applies regardless of your level or prestige in the company.

Express quiet enthusiasm, and withhold excessive comment. Your new peers want you to appreciate what they have done, and your superiors will take pleasure in knowing that you enjoy your job. After all, your enthusiasm was surely one of the chief attributes that got you hired. But if you act too effusively you risk annoying your colleagues. Keep your enthusiasm moderate, and make your approving comments genuine: "I'd like to hear more about how you came up with that direct-mail flyer; it seems right on target to me." Or "This is one of the best designs I've seen in a long time."

Being on time for meetings, proffering information to fill in the gaps, volunteering to try to solve a problem within your expertise, or showing appreciation for an invitation or gratuitous bit of advice are among the many ways to communicate your enthusiasm. Just don't overdo it.

Survey for the best resources, to help you do your job. It is easy to become isolated in a new job, feeling that you must prove yourself on your own. Do not fall into this trap. It's possible to get others to help you without being a pest. They will enjoy giving guidance, as long as you don't ask the same question twice.

When the tools to accomplish a particular task aren't readily available, ask your co-workers, your boss, or people in other departments who might have faced similar assignments. Read up on the subject in professional journals, at libraries, or go to other organizations dealing with the same issue. Plug in the good surveying skills that got you this position in the first place.

Don't hesitate to seek answers from others, because without the right information you won't be able to deliver a satisfactory result. Just remind yourself of the number-one tenet of gathering information: You must know exactly what you're looking for.

Deliver superb work in a timely manner. Just remember the old axiom: You have only one opportunity to make a first impression.

You are in a job *you* selected, doing what *you* want to do. Get ahead of the game by going out of your way to deliver a polished product, whether it be a report, speech, design, sales tool, or a new way of resolving customer problems. If a good result requires a team effort, create a team and give the team credit.

If possible, deliver your results early, but not too early. (You don't want to give the impression that it's too easy!)

The pleasure of watching you perform well, with enthusiasm, creates a lasting impression on your boss. You may have to withstand a few slings and arrows from jealous colleagues, but remind yourself that you are competing with yourself—not against someone else—which helps you to display the right attitude. You want to best your own record. When you are good at your own job, you can help others, which makes you look even better.

Make a Date With Yourself

Establish regular life-review sessions that take place every six months or so. Perhaps now is the right time for your first one. Jot down stories describing your recent activities and identify the skills you used. The first story you want to document is how you got your new job. No doubt you developed some new skills in the course of securing it.

In adding to your life stories, remember to use all the pointers in Chapters 3 through 6. As you identify skills, add them to your clusters, or begin to form new ones. And always continue to coach yourself on how to talk about what you have done. Remember to describe the *difference* you made in each situation.

Once you've completed this life-review session, make a date with yourself on your calendar for six months from now.

Keep on Surveying

Make surveying a way of life. You will only get better and better at it. Whenever you need a refresher, look back at Chapters 12 through 16. Surveying is your most important business tool; it is also an important personal tool. Whether you are trying to understand a customer's greatest needs or to find the best way to learn conversational Chinese, it's all the same process. In addition to leading you to sound decisions, surveying widens your circle of friends and professional contacts, making future surveying easier. You will know people in all walks of life willing to talk to you about their areas of expertise.

Continue to design your survey plans, at least in your mind. The discipline of thinking out a specific topic and pertinent questions translates directly into all manner of business projects.

Look to the Future

Once a year, take part of a day to review and polish your goals. The day could be your birthday, New Year's Day, the anniversary of the day you got hired, just before your annual review—any day that seems to mark a new beginning for you. Read over Chapters 7 through 10, and enjoy some of the exercises again as though you were doing them for the first time. You may want to change a word or two in your goals statement to make it even more meaningful for you.

Determine Your Objectives

Revise and update your plan of action at least once a year. A good time to do so is right after your annual review of goals. Assess your old objectives and set new ones for the next year. Remember, it's better to take small achievable steps than to attempt to make giant changes.

Include both personal and business objectives in your plans; often the two will intertwine. You may determine that you want to purchase a house at the beach in two years, which means that you will have to increase your sales targets 3 percent beyond the norm. Don't set the objective, however, unless you can devise a realistic plan to do it.

Keep your plan of action in front of you throughout the year, and frequently check your progress, noting if you need to revise or redouble your efforts. This involves a certain amount of discipline, but it is worth it if it helps you achieve your goals.

The Last Word

Remain true to your dreams. They are now represented within your goals and plan of action. That is one reason it is so helpful to keep them in front of you, revising them as you grow and learn. They celebrate who you are and encourage you to operate according to the values and aims that are most meaningful to you. Your success depends upon knowing and acting according to the reality of your interests and abilities as well as the reality of your environment. You will prosper when you link this knowledge to your energy.

APPENDICES

Tips on Getting (and Staying) Organized

J UST AS WITH any project, it's important to be organized while you're engaged in the Crystal-Barkley process. You'll be creating quite a few documents and doing a fair amount of research, including meeting with several potential employers, all of which will be much easier to manage if you have a pleasant workspace and an orderly filing system. Following are tips on what you need and how to organize it.

Your "Office"

You need a space to call your own during this endeavor. Most people don't have the luxury of an extra room to use exclusively as an office. Next best is a corner of a quiet room. Be sure that you choose a spot with electrical outlets and a telephone jack nearby. (Unless you have great reception in your area, stick to regular, rather than cordless telephones.)

> *Being organized can spell the difference between opportunities seized and opportunities missed.*

Buy or borrow a desk or table at a good writing height if you don't have one already; add a typing table or computer stand and a comfortable desk chair. Incandescent lighting and daylight (if possible) are easiest on the eyes. Finally, make sure you have at least one file cabinet in which to organize your materials. (A sufficiently deep drawer of a bureau will also work.)

Do whatever you can to make your office space comfortable and attractive. Hang a favorite picture or photograph on the wall, and place a nice rug underfoot. Buy a pretty plant or treat yourself to flowers. You will spend many hours here, and you should enjoy them as much as possible.

A Telephone Line

Your telephone is your lifeline. Installing a second line isn't necessary as long as your telephone is always answered properly. If other people in the household share the phone line, request that everyone cooperate by answering the phone courteously. Place notepads and pencils by each telephone so others can easily take messages for you. For the time being, make sure that any children in your house never answer the telephone. A child screaming, "It's for you again!" is rarely the best introduction to new business contacts.

Do not get "call waiting" and if you have it, cancel it at least temporarily. Call waiting forces you to interrupt conversations, often at most inopportune moments. Choose voice mail instead, which will answer your phone when you are on another call and when you are not there. You can check your messages just as you do with an answering machine or service.

Must-Have Supplies

Office supply stores can be very tempting, but fortunately you don't need every hand-dandy gadget available. Here are the essentials you should have to get the maximum in efficiency.

- 1 three-ring binder, with paper and tab dividers
- Six pocket-sized notebooks
- Colored markers and highlighters
- Expansion files, $\frac{1}{2}$ dozen
- File folders, 1 box
- Small blank cards (the size of business cards, but of cheaper stock)
- 5" x 7" index cards, 6 dozen
- 5" x 7" note cards (buff or white) with your name printed, centered, at the top; matching envelopes with address printed on back flap
- Letterhead 8½" x 11" in buff, light grey, or white; your name, address, telephone number printed at top center. Matching envelopes, with address in the upper left or centered on the back flap
- Business cards
- Large month-at-a-glance calendar
- Small week-at-a-glance appointment book or electronic calendar
- Rolodex or electronic address system for your desk
- Briefcase or leather folder for meetings

Organizing Your Surveys

You will need one expansion folder for each survey. In it you'll keep everything related to the survey.

■ For each survey subject, maintain lists of articles or abstracts you want to read; books you want to read; possible contact names and addresses, gleaned from research; issues, trends, problems, or opportunities concerning your survey subject. File these lists under separate headings (Research/Reading Lists, Possible Contacts, Issues and Problems, etc.) in your expansion folder.

■ Access to computer databases is available at most university and public libraries. A research librarian can help orient you to various sources of on-line information. But before you go on-line, do some basic research first to at least pin down your specific topic (see Chapters 12 and 14); otherwise, you will become bogged down in endless extraneous information, which wastes time and money. Also, the more focused you are, the more help a research librarian can give you. On-line searches can save you a lot of time as opposed to print research, but only if you know exactly what you want.

■ List in your Rolodex or in a computer file the name, address, phone, and fax numbers of each person you plan to see, along with the names of secretaries and/or assistants.

■ Type your notes from each meeting on a single sheet of paper, and file it in a slot in your expansion folder called "Meeting Notes." If you see more than one person in a single organization, create a separate sheet for each one. File correspondence separately.

Making the Best Use of Your Time

We all have times of day when we're more "on" than others. To a certain extent, you can and should organize your time to take advantage of your personal internal clock. On the other hand, there are some schedules you will have to adhere to, regardless of personal preference.

■ Get up early, whether you are a morning person or not. Most of the world begins work in the morning.

■ If you're not currently working outside your home, get dressed and go to your desk, as though you had a job to get to.

■ If you are a night person, try to schedule most of your meetings for the late morning, when going out and about will energize you. Do your desk work later in the day, when it's easy for you to stay alert.

■ If you are a morning person, do the opposite.

■ Avoid working late into the night unless you absolutely have to. Even if you are a night owl, working late tends to ruin the next day.

■ Plan occasional breaks and small rewards—listening to a piece of music you love, walking around the block a few times, calling a friend for a social date.

■ Consider when the people you are calling are likely to be most receptive. If you're trying to talk to a salesperson, for instance, don't call first thing Monday morning—that's when sales meetings are most commonly held. Don't even think of calling people in the theater until noon (they've likely been performing the night before.) Late afternoon is a good time to contact stockbrokers but an impossible time to reach athletic coaches.

Keeping Yourself on Schedule

At the end of each day, review your plan for the next. Do the same at the end of each week and the end of each month. Use the month-at-a-glance calendar to select blocks of time in which to accomplish particular activities; set your deadlines, taking into account holidays and social engagements that may affect scheduling. Use the week-at-a-glance calendar to keep track of specific appointments and daily activities.

Be ready to take advantage of any bits of extra time that come your way. Carry your pocket notebook everywhere you go. While you are waiting for an appointment or are in transit write down your notes, make lists, and compose your thoughts for letters and proposals.

The Power of Goals

Any system of organization is merely a means to fulfill an end. Remember, *you* work the system; don't let the system work you! Your personal goals statement (see Chapter 10) is the primary motivator to keep you moving and on track. Post your goals statement in your "office" in plain sight. Start and end each day by reading it. Your goals statement provides steady encouragement that will boost your spirits and renew your energy every day.

How to Handle the Standard Interview

NTERVIEW! THE WORD can induce paralysis, or at least sweaty palms. It conjures images of an interviewer holding all the cards and the interviewee struggling to say the right thing and stay in the game. All too often the power differential is such that as the interviewee, we feel vulnerable and defensive—clearly not in a frame of mind to show ourselves to our best advantage.

Fortunately, if you have carefully followed the system laid out in this handbook, you are not going to be in many—or any—"standard interviews." Instead you'll be setting up proposal meetings, which have a very different feel to them, because you already know the people you are seeing and the organizations you are approaching.

Sometimes, however, standard interviews do come along in spite of your intentions to handle the matter differently: A headhunter calls, you respond to an irresistible ad, a friend urges you to contact an organization he or she knows, you go to see campus recruiters, or you have become involved in a large corporation or academic or governmental organization in which there seems no way around "that interview."

If you seriously subscribe to Crystal-Barkley principles, you will turn the typical interview into one of two types of meetings: a survey or a combination survey and proposal meeting.

You will turn it into a survey meeting if you still feel unsure about your interest in the organization considering you. This is a good chance for you to find out more. You will want to reread the material in Chapters 12 and 14 and have a sound survey plan in mind.

If you have already surveyed a lot, you may feel certain you are on the right track. If you've studied the organization, you can use the first part of the interview to verify your information by asking some additional survey questions and use the last part to make your proposal (consult Chapters 16 and 17 and this appendix).

Whichever course you choose, the only way to make the impression you want is to prepare. Don't even think of winging it. Even if you are going into a series of interviews that seem to be variations on the same theme, prepare for each one as though it were the only one.

Ten Steps to a Positive Interview

1. Assess where you are in the Crystal-Barkley process: How much do you know about your skills? How sure do you feel about your direction? Do you have enough information to know whether the organization you are interviewing with should even be among your targets?

2. Check out the organization (and the field, if it is new to you) in the library and call everyone you know who might be knowledgeable on the subject. Make note of specific accomplishments or groundbreaking work the organization or individual you will see has achieved. This equips you to say something honestly flattering at the beginning of the interview and impress the interviewer with the fact that you have done your homework. You would be surprised how many people neglect this obvious step.

3. Review your Talking Papers. You want to have examples of results you have achieved using your particular skills on the tip of your tongue. If you haven't done your Talking Papers yet, pick examples directly from your life stories that show how you changed and improved situations and what skills you used in these efforts. (See Chapters 2 and 5.)

4. Imagine the needs this organization and this person are likely to have in relation to what you are prepared to do. Take time with this. Then write down the questions you think the interviewer might ask you.

5. Ask a friend to role-play the interview with you. Give him the questions you think may be asked and tell him who he is supposed to be. (Believe us, the actual interview will feel much easier. If you do well in the role-play, you will do very well in the interview.)

6. Without jumping to conclusions, think about the likely goals and values of the organization based on what you have learned from your research. Be prepared to draw analogies to people or circumstances you are familiar with and genuinely admire. For example:

> "I see that you run your firm like Roy Vagelos ran Merck, with more regard for the firm's long-term health than for the short-term effect you might have on the company's stock price."

Interviewers are very concerned about compatibility, or "fit," and this is one way to demonstrate you are of a similar mind (if you are; if you aren't, faking it will only lead to unhappiness down the road. Better to let this one go by or view it as an interim job.)

7. Connect your answers to the actual needs and work at hand. Use examples from your experience that are most relevant. Examples from personal, nonworking experiences and early childhood can also be convincing and relevant. For example, if part of the job's responsibility is making presentations or lobbying activity you might say something like this:

> "Ever since I was a kid, my family says I was on my soapbox, and in high school I enjoyed competing on the debating team."

8. Devise an actual written proposal (see Chapter 16) based on what you know about the company's needs so far. You may not follow this exactly, but it will give you a framework for describing to an interviewer what you can do for him or her as a person as well as what you can do for the organization.

9. The night before and the day of the interview, close your eyes for a few minutes. Create a picture in your mind of the interview; picture yourself relaxed and confident, responding to questions and asking questions of your own. See yourself getting up to leave the interview and the interviewer saying exactly what you want to be said. Literally imagine the words you will hear from the interviewer. *No kidding, it works!*

10. Make sure you have clear directions to the interview location and plan to arrive a few minutes early. Use your extra time to assess the atmosphere, talk with a receptionist, check out publications in the anteroom, and pick up any other background information you can.

Interviews with positive outcomes boil down to your having four very important pieces of information in hand:

■ What skills you are equipped to offer

■ What you want to accomplish in a job

■ What constitutes acceptable working circumstances (hours, benefits, working conditions, pay)

■ What the employer is likely to want and need

What Interviewers Are After

Everyone who is considering paying you to do something wants to know the following.

■ **Can you do the job?** (Do you have the skills, aptitude, and experience they believe the job requires?)

■ **Will you do the job?** (Do you have the motivation and interest in the particular tasks at hand?)

■ **Will you fit in?** (Will you accept the organization's way of doing things and get along well with co-workers and customers?)

■ **Will the economics of hiring you work?** (Can the organization gain more by having you than it takes to pay you?)

Responding to Standard Interview Questions

Get into the mindset: Every question is an opportunity to demonstrate how you are the right person for the job. Focus your responses on contributions you can make and be prepared to back up every assertion with an example from your own life history that proves you can do it.

Questions will vary according to your age and experience. Recent college grads are more likely than experienced workers to be confronted with "trick" questions such as:

■ "Where do you see yourself in five years?"

■ "What are your career goals?"

■ "How does this position relate to your career goals?"

■ "Describe your ideal job."

■ "Why did you choose this career?"

However, no matter where you are in your career it's always a good idea to be prepared for these questions, since many have double meanings. For instance, if you are asked **"Where do you want to be in five years?"** the hidden question is "Are you drifting into the first job that you can find, or is this company one you've selected?"

Standard interview questions are typically grouped into categories aimed at discovering your:

- Personal characteristics
- Goals
- Education
- Experience
- Compatibility
- Compensation expectations

Personal Questions

The reason personal questions are asked is to discover your attitude toward work and your typical behavior. Through these, the interviewer is trying to determine if you are a good fit with the organization and the people who are already in it.

Although personal questions intimidate many people, they actually present an excellent opportunity to communicate the information about yourself you most want to get across. The extremely open-ended nature of personal questions allows you to move directly into what you believe most qualifies you for the job at hand.

"Tell me about yourself" gives the interviewer an opportunity to observe how well you organize your thoughts. You might be tempted to start with, "I graduated from college in 1980 and went to work for"—and then continue with a chronology of your work experience to date. Well, don't do that.

Instead say, "I am someone who has always had an interest in (whatever is the main job function)." Then proceed to describe how you have increased your knowledge of this function by means of two or three (no more) examples from your life history.

Use examples in which you really made a difference. Remember, you are not only being tested on how well you measure up in relation to the job's central functions, but how well you organize and communicate your thoughts. Thus, your response demonstrates your communication skills and (perhaps more important) your confidence in what you are saying. You can see why you can't risk rambling or presenting disjointed thoughts.

"Tell me about yourself" is also used to determine how well you handle pressure and is typically asked first. Other ways of asking the same question are:

- "Why should we hire you?"
- "What can you do for us?"
- "What are your greatest strengths?"
- "How would you describe yourself?"
- "What do you believe is unique about you?" (This one can stop you in your tracks if you're unprepared!)

Here's how Elizabeth and David responded to such questions. Note how they emphasize their strengths and interests.

Elizabeth: "Ever since I was a young girl I have been fascinated by history and art, and I have had a knack for converting this interest into highly readable commentary. I was invited to publish my college thesis on the role of women as depicted in medieval tapestries and paintings as a series of articles in the alumni magazine. I later paid for a summer in Europe by writing travel pieces on medieval towns in Italy, France, and Spain."

David: "One of my greatest talents is quickly establishing a congenial and cohesive atmosphere in a group learning situation. I must have a dozen letters from people in groups I have led commenting on how pleased they were at how much was accomplished and how they made new friends in the process."

When asked **"What are your greatest weaknesses?"** the temptation is usually to say too much. The idea is to demonstrate that you have a realistic view of yourself without revealing a weakness that would do you real harm in the job. If you worked through the early chapters of this handbook, you learned how to concentrate exclusively on your strengths, and you realize that leading from strength, not from weakness, wins the day. So, answer by picking something that you are less good at but working to improve. For instance:

> "I am presently working to increase my proficiency with computer graphics so that I can enhance the visual components of the presentations I make."

Perhaps you can give a recent example of how you have improved your behavior or capacity:

> "I recently created some charts by computer that everyone thought added a lot of pizzazz to my sales presentation."

Another route is to pick a good quality that, if used to excess, might be considered a weakness.

> "I tend to be impatient for results; I am learning to hold back a bit so as to accommodate others' working styles."

"What do you think is your greatest achievement to date?" Focus on an achievement directly related to the position you are discussing. You can explain that this is what you are doing.

> "I don't know whether this is my greatest achievement, but it is one I am very proud of and it may be of interest to you. We were having what seemed to be intractable problems getting our new fabric off the looms without flaws. I ended up getting the loom manufacturer, our foreman, and the people on the line in a meeting together, and we solved the problem by a loom adjustment. It required us to halt manufacturing overnight while we met to solve the problem. Our hourly workers said this was the first time they had been asked to participate in a management-level meeting. We not only eliminated the flaws, but we also created a new spirit on the floor."

"How well do you handle pressure?" Answer very specifically here, not with a generalization like, "Oh, fine!" Give examples related to your previous work that illustrate how you held up under pressure. This is the only way you will be believable. The question may also be asked as, "How successful are you at meeting tight deadlines?"

It's especially important for older workers to answer these questions accurately and forcefully, as employers sometimes worry that an older person will not have the energy of a young worker to address the extra demands of a pressured situation. Say what's true for you and draw from your experience.

"When I was responsible for developing advertising campaigns for clients, it was common to face one- or two-week deadlines. I made sure our team used every tool available to speed up our work and enhance our creativity. We held daily strategy meetings to ensure that we would have time to review and modify our work. Often we worked into the evening and on the weekends. I found I could be very effective in this mode for reasonable periods of time."

Perhaps your own response would be even more personal:

"I know I work best under pressure. When faced with a deadline for presentations, I always seem to go into high gear: The presentation gets prepared, and everything else gets done too."

When the interviewer asks, **"How do you solve problems?"** you are really being quizzed on how well your style matches the preferred style in the organization and the demands of the job. If you've had a chance to survey the organization, you may already have a good idea of its internal behavior patterns. Ideally your answer will reflect your own style and also suit that of the organization.

Assess what you are likely to be getting into. For example, some jobs or situations call for a team effort in solving problems and some require instant, independent judgment. But don't pretend to be someone you're not. This is one area where you can get into big trouble. Suppose you're someone who prefers to act only after careful deliberation. This method of decision-making can be ideal in some situations and produce disastrous results in others. There's simply no substitute for knowing yourself in this regard.

For example, you might explain that you like to study a situation and clearly define the problem before rushing to a solution. But if this is an organization with an electric atmosphere—such as a television newsroom or the trading floor of a brokerage house—you must also provide evidence of how you can move fast.

Questions Related to Goals

When you are asked about your goals or aims in life, the interviewer wants to know two things: whether you in fact have goals and, if you do, whether they match those of the enterprise.

People who have clear goals are generally motivated and productive. If your goals match the organization's, an employer is likely to be very anxious to have you on board. Following are some often-asked questions:

- Where do you see yourself in five years? Ten years?

- Why did you choose this career?

- What are your career goals?

- Describe your ideal job.

- What do you want to accomplish in life at this point?

- How does your interest in this position relate to your career goals?

Again, it's best to be honest about your goals. A blatant declaration of commitment to the organization's known goals will sound as though you are just trying to impress the interviewer and don't know yourself very well. The best responses show that you have devoted some time to thinking out your own goals and know that they are congruent with the organization's. Show your commitment to fulfilling both your own goals and theirs! Here are some examples of how other people have successfully answered these kinds of questions:

"Tell me about any specific objectives you have set for yourself for the next 10 years."

> "I can't honestly say that I have an exact timetable, but I do have a clear picture of what I want and how I would like to accomplish it. I want to provide information and advice to farmers on subjects ranging from farm management to soil conservation. This means I must be up to date on research and legislation, maintain an ongoing education program for myself in agriculture and business, and work in situations that will challenge my learning skills as well as my ability to do the job."

"I would like to play an active role in designing software that has high utility in the health-care field. I have always cared a lot about world health problems, and I am determined to have an impact on them by using my skills in software development and planning. This organization seems admirably placed to have a far-reaching effect."

"Why did you choose this career?"

"I have been interested in broadcast journalism for a long time, partly because I am fascinated by breaking news and also because I know I have the ability to speak to the public in a conversational way. It is important to me to work with a first-rate broadcast organization that shares my desire and has the capacity to get news on the air as it is happening rather than after the fact."

"Describe your ideal job."

"It will be one in which I am given latitude to provide the customer with the most wholesome food possible at moderate prices. I am resourceful at purchasing and would love to be turned loose to source and purchase foods that are not only the highest quality but also the best price."

"How does your interest in this position relate to your goals?"

"Working as a veterinary assistant would enable me to do two things: work with and help animals, which is what I want to do with my life, and discover whether veterinary work is the way I want to do it. I know I understand animals and can calm them when they're scared, and I'm also very organized and meticulous—attributes that I hope would be helpful in my work with the doctors."

The best responses to goal-centered questions draw on your own values, interests, and top skills. You make these relevant to the organization by showing how they match its needs. Always describe the kind of work you want to do rather than stating a job title you want. Better to say, "I see myself using my managerial talents helping teachers to be more effective," rather than, "I want to be a high school principal."

Questions Related to Education

Younger job seekers or those seeking highly technical positions will be faced with more education-related questions than older job seekers. If older people are asked such questions, they can make them an opportunity to emphasize their enthusiasm for lifelong learning, which is an impressive characteristic. Here are some questions you might hear and examples to inspire your responses:

"Do you have plans for additional education?" The interviewer is trying to find out whether you see this line of work as part of a long-term commitment as opposed to a stop-gap measure. If you do have plans for additional education, be specific about what you want to learn and how an employer could possibly benefit.

> "The longer I am in management, the more I recognize how much I can learn from the behavioral sciences to enhance my effectiveness and that of those under me. I will definitely want to take some related workshops and courses."

> "Three or four years into this job, I would like to consider working toward a graduate degree in the evenings. I'd like to find out whether the company encourages employees to continue their educations by offering tuition reimbursement programs or flexible hours."

"Do you feel that your grades are a good indication of your aptitude in this area?" (Or a host of similar questions regarding grade point average.) A good answer, regardless of how stunning your GPA was, might be:

> "Like most people, I suppose, I've always done best at what I liked the most, which is one of the many reasons I find this company's work so exciting and am very pleased to be talking with you about this position."

If you had really low grades, mention any extenuating circumstances, such as working while in school or caring for an ill parent. Tell how you worked to correct the situation and call attention to skills that aren't reflected in the subjects in which you had poor grades. Above all, move on to another subject before you say too much.

"What were your favorite subjects and why?" This should be easy; just be sure you make your response relevant to the job that needs doing. Also, make some reference to the more broadly based skills that you have, such as problem-solving, communicating, or writing entertainingly. For example:

> "I guess it's obvious math must have been a favorite of mine since I did well in it and now want to function as a financial officer. What might not be so obvious is that I apparently have some talent for solving other kinds of problems: I came up with a plan for my fraternity to advantageously sell some property it had been left in a will."

"How well do you think school has prepared you for this type of work?" Here you are being given a chance to display your understanding of the job. If your major area of study is appropriate, great. If not, concentrate on how you learned the skills which are directly related to the job. One MBA applying for a job coordinating and distributing health services described how her business class team scored the best on a competition to build a fledgling airline.

> "One of the best times I had in business school was working with my team on a simulated airline business start-up. The team used my approach to scheduling and assigning planes to our terminal cities, and they credited me with our win. I think many of the same factors would be present in the distribution of health services, just in a different environment."

"Why did you choose that college?" The interviewer is trying to learn something of your decision-making style. Briefly describe what went into your decision: academic reputation, extracurricular activities, geography, atmosphere, and so forth. Above all, emphasize how the school fit into your goals. If you did a poor job of choosing, explain what you learned from this and how you would do it differently again.

> "In truth, soccer was the main reason I chose La Grange, but I soon realized that I had to have more depth in geology and mapping. I transferred to Southwestern U, which was a great decision."

What About Your Experience?

When an interviewer asks, **"What is your experience?"** you are being asked to *prove* you can do the work. The interviewer doesn't want to be blamed if you fail at the job, so this is an important part of the interview when evidence is going to be recorded to back up the decision to hire you.

If you have done similar work before, say so and describe the circumstances. If you have little or no experience in the field you are now trying to enter, the key is to display your understanding of the actual functions that need to be performed in this job and show how your skills transfer to them.

Occasionally you'll discover that the employer is looking for a different mix of skills than those traditionally associated with the job. For example, an ad agency starting to create on-line ads will desperately need designers with up-to-the-minute computer graphic skills.

The key is to be relevant. Remember, what the interviewer thinks is needed is what counts. The best way to find this out is to have done some research in advance. The next best way is to have asked intelligent questions during the meeting. Let your enthusiasm show; enthusiasm as well as experience can convince. For example, a supervisor from an automaker's plant can score big with an electronics firm that seems to be headed for labor problems.

> "One of the skills I enjoy using is bringing management's mandates to workers on the line without creating a confrontation. This sounds like it could be useful given the recent union vote at your Fall River plant."

"Why did you leave your last (or why are you leaving your current) job?" This means "How long are you likely to stay here? How stable are you? How easily will opportunities lure you away? Are you a problem worker?"

If you were fired or part of a general layoff, you may be nervous about how to respond. But these conditions have lost much of their previous stigma, so be honest about it—briefly. Don't put down yourself or your former employer. Chalk the experience up to a difference in temperaments or goals, and quickly move to the positive reasons why you are talking to this new organization, without seeming to avoid the issue. The less said the better. Go on to concentrate on the positive: why you want to be there and why it is a good thing for them for you to be there.

If you left for voluntary reasons, explain them, but be sure to say why you're interested in the new job. If you're presently employed, give a few reasons why you're ready to leave, and again bring the focus back to the new job, as the candidate below did.

> "I've simply gotten to the point where I feel I have contributed all I want to, given my current company's product positioning. You are ideally poised to take advantage of the expansion of U.S. markets throughout Asia. Given my knowledge of Chinese as well as retail foods, you were naturally one of my foremost targets for work. It would be very exciting and challenging to be part of your entry into the Chinese market."

Or, it may be that you have a personal reason for the move: to be nearer ailing parents, or perhaps your spouse got a terrific opportunity. It's fine to mention these reasons, but couple them with some positive contribution you want to make to this employer.

"Can you provide references?" Well, of course! You have to be ready to respond to this promptly. Even though previous employers are usually extremely guarded (for legal reasons) about what they will say about you, most new employers do check references. Try to choose people who will speak highly about your abilities and commitment. It's smart to contact all your potential references in advance and ask their permission to give their names.

Compatibility Questions

"Why are you interested in this company (firm, organization)?" Here's where your enthusiasm and knowledge about this particular organization will distinguish you. If you are asked this question, presumably you will have had some time to do some research on the organization. At a minimum, you should have asked around about the company and read its annual report and/or any other printed materials it produces. Ideally you will also have had time to go to the library to look up articles about it and its competition.

Concentrate on the values and goals of the organization when you describe your interest. Blend genuine compliments with your own qualifications to produce an attractive response:

> "Your reputation for fairness in the marketplace is well known and a big motivator to me. I felt your recall of your last year's model was extremely well handled from the customer's point of view."

> "Your goal of producing cost estimates with less than a 5 percent error margin seems unique in the construction industry, and I'd like to be part of such an effort."

> "This seems to me to be the premier organization for researching the genetic disposition to viral disease, and I have been preparing myself for some time to meet your high standards."

"Under what conditions do you work best?" If you have followed the Crystal-Barkley process you will know exactly what working conditions are most pleasant and productive for you. Before the interview, refer to Chapter 6 to get your thoughts in order. Questions that may be asked to get at similar information are:

- "What motivates you to do your best work?"
- "How do you want to be supervised?"
- "What are your most productive hours of the day?"
- "How many hours a day do you think you should work?"
- "Do you work better in a team or solo?"
- "How do you feel about travel?"
- "Are you willing to relocate?"
- "How do you feel about routine versus project work?"

Definitely discuss the working conditions that are most important to you, and if things are going well, include some that are less important. This is not the place to equivocate. We know that if employees cannot satisfy their most important workplace criteria, neither they nor the hiring organization will prosper by their employment.

"Do you have trouble getting along with any particular type of person?" Here the interviewer is trying to find out whether you'll "fit in" with the organization. Even if you have the talent, you won't be at your most productive if you don't get along with the rest of the staff. The interviewer will be gauging your fit more by observing you than by your response to this question, but your answer is still important.

The interviewer knows that it's impossible to create a situation in which you get along perfectly with everyone. So, in replying, focus on *traits* which you reject or avoid (see Chapter 6) and give an example of how you worked to resolve some difficult situations when these issues were involved.

> "I recall once having a supervisor who was constantly looking over my shoulder, correcting my work and telling me what to do as I was working. It was so distracting that I felt I couldn't get the work done on schedule. I finally devised a system of scheduled morning and afternoon reviews to satisfy his need for control and yet leave me freedom to get the work done. We gradually became comfortable with each other and reduced the check-in reviews to twice a week."

"Is there anything you dislike about the sound of this job?" Watch out, trick question! The interviewer actually wants to see if you will dodge it. Shift the emphasis from "dislike" to "concern," and then bring up an issue that would concern any thinking person determined to succeed. For example, if you are interviewing for a teaching position, you might say you are concerned that the classes are larger than you think they ought to be. Then take the edge off your comment by remarking that you welcome the challenge, if you do!

Compensation Questions

Salary and other compensation questions often come up early in standard interviews. This is the worst time to discuss them, because it is when you and your interviewer know least about each other. The best way to handle this sensitive question is covered in Chapter 17.

If you are acting as an independent consultant or contractor, make a private budget and a little business plan (for your eyes only) before getting into discussions of compensation. Failure to do this is one of the several reasons people working independently or starting their own small businesses often don't make ends meet. You must do for yourself what you would be required to do for an employer if you were responsible for a business unit.

Remember, in this situation you are responsible for your own overhead: a place to work and the utilities to keep it open, equipment and supplies, and health insurance. You must also somehow support the time you are out selling and not actually working for a client. Most employers understand this when independent contractors quote their fee structures. When you can back up your fees with sensible explanations (if asked), it is one more sign that you are a competent business person.

To Sum Up

You can see that preparation is your best ally when handling a standard interview. Even though your odds of a successful conclusion are lower than if you were making a full-fledged proposal to a potential employer (with other possible employers in the wings), you can do much better for yourself by using any time you have before the interview to do your homework on yourself and the employer's needs.

However the interview ends, always try to leave a friend behind. Making a favorable impression, even if you do not fill the requirements for the current opening, may lead you to be thought of for a future position, or even referred to a colleague. A standard interview is one more opportunity to extend your network of contacts and add to the cadre of people working within your area of interest who know and respect you.

FROM RESUMES TO PROPOSALS

A N IN-PERSON PROPOSAL, presented orally, is always the preferred method to make the case for your next job. This route doesn't involve providing a resume—you present your credentials within your proposal. But there usually comes a time when you must back up what you have said on paper. The *least effective* written presentation is a chronological resume; the *most effective* is a well-thought-out, well-documented proposal. In between are several options. We'll take you through each one, from least to most effective. (We are not providing examples of less effective resumes because we do not recommend them; however, if you feel you must develop one of these resumes and need guidance, there are many books on the subject available in bookstores and libraries, and on-line services have many reference materials too.)

Chronological Resume

The most traditional (and outmoded) resume dispassionately lists your work experience and education, starting with the present and going backward in time. Under "Work Experience," dates appear on the left, positions in the right column. A sentence or two explains your responsibilities and outlines your accomplishments directly related to the job you are seeking. If you held two or more similar jobs, focus on something different in each.

Under "Education" list your most advanced degree first (go back only as far as college). You may include specialized training, naming the training institution, dates attended, and certification, if any. If you have no college or specialized training, do not include any educational information on your resume. If you are still in college, give credits earned so far and grade point average, if impressive. Also include leadership roles, and extracurricular activities pertinent to the position at hand.

If you wish, include a "Personal Information" section at the end of the resume, which can include voluntary activities, special awards, professional affiliations, military service, languages, and any pastimes or hobbies that have specific relevance to the employer or position.

You can shape even this limited format to respond to the specific needs of a particular employer simply by accentuating particular work experiences and accomplishments.

Curriculum Vitae

A curriculum vitae (or CV) is commonly used in the academic world, and offers a simple listing, without embellishment, of positions held; speeches (title, where, when, and to whom); publications (date, publisher); awards; and degrees. It is also organized chronologically, starting with the present. A CV can be useful to accompany proposals and is simply handy to have around in case you need it.

Functional Resume

A functional resume is organized by function—administration, leadership, traffic management, planning—rather than by chronology, though it usually describes where and when these tasks took place. Functional resumes are sometimes used by candidates who wish to change career fields or who have spotty employment records. Because most skills are transferable, this kind of resume allows you to demonstrate the necessary abilities for the job in question.

The problem with this type of resume is that while it tells much more about the writer, it can be difficult to comprehend. If a potential employer has to dig too hard to figure out what you actually did, the resume will hit the discard pile. So if you choose this type of resume, don't try to be clever. Be very specific and clear, and write without embellishment.

Begin by stating your employment objective. Then offer your experience within broad categories of the functions you have performed. For instance: coaching, teaching, managing, and so forth. Within each category, explain what you did, for what organization, and when. Emphasize your accomplishments and any recognition received. Education and personal information may also be included at the end.

Biographical Sketch

A biographical sketch is not really a resume, but it covers some of the same territory. It's usually sent only after you have established a personal rapport with a potential employer. You might send it along with one of the other pieces described here. Its advantage is that it is flexible enough to include interesting side notes that would be hard to fit into more structured formats.

The purpose of a biographical sketch is to describe how and why your experience is suited to the employer's needs. A biographical sketch is not something you can expect to knock off in a few minutes. Be prepared to devote time to developing and writing a solid piece of prose about yourself. Start by looking back through your activities from the skills and life stories chapters (Chapters 2, 3, and 4), and selecting descriptions that apply directly to your potential employer's needs. The idea is to emphasize the skills, aptitudes, personal characteristics, and experiences that support your work objective, showing the employer that you are the right candidate. The sketch should always begin and end with your strongest points.

Here's an example from a young woman hoping to get involved in producing special events.

Nancy K. Loomis
554 Newtown Parkway
Rye, NY 02112
914-287-0234

BIOGRAPHICAL SKETCH

From her earliest days, Nancy Loomis has been involved in producing events and greeting the public in ways that have been highly entertaining for everyone concerned. Raised in Florida, the daughter of a scientist and an engineer, her creative turn of mind has been complemented by her disciplined upbringing and a B.S. in hotel/restaurant management from Florida International University.

Foremost among Nancy's accomplishments while still in school was her spearheading the establishment of a new chapter of a national sorority on campus. She managed to enlist the support of students and the administration, form committees to handle the logistics, attract an initial membership of 27 women, and simultaneously maintain a grade point average that put her in the upper half of her class. In the course of promoting the sorority's aims, Nancy learned to enjoy making presentations and orchestrating events both large and small.

Nancy held many paid and volunteer jobs before and during college. In fact, her family dubbed her the "bionic kid" because of the energy level she displayed in pursuing her interests. From acting in several lead roles with a little theater group to teaching at a local summer camp for children with physical disabilites, she found she enjoyed the fruits of long hours of work.

There have been many occasions for Nancy to demonstrate her project-management and events-planning talents: proposing and mounting fashion shows for a local women's apparel shop, which increased the store's sales by 10 percent in the same month; assisting the manager of a popular, often crowded gourmet restaurant; devising an effective special events logistics control system for a major hotel as assistant manager in her first job out of college; successfully introducing prospective students to her university (better than 70 percent acceptance and registration achieved); and participating in team sports as well as teaching them. Prior to college, Nancy participated in Junior Achievement and was CEO one year.

Nancy has always been interested in cooking. In 1990 she completed a Chaine des Rotisseurs cooking program, and she is often host to her friends. She is a cross country skiing, tennis, and swimming enthusiast and enjoys excellent health.

Nancy is currently working with a talent agency and is researching the most productive ways to put to work her ideas on promoting business for ski resorts through special events.

Qualifications Brief

A qualifications brief is an enhanced version of the functional resume. It's tailored for a specific employer and is a very focused document. This background piece still takes second place to a proposal, but it does allow you to present yourself quite fairly. Sending a qualifications brief is a good solution when someone insists on receiving a resume before setting up a proposal meeting.

Begin by stating a clear, specific work objective—a concise, interesting explanation of what you want to do for the organization. Everything else on the page flows from this objective, justifies it, and supports it.

The next section deals with your qualifications to carry out your objective; it describes experience that provides direct evidence that you can meet the objective you are proposing.

You may close with education and personal information sections. If relevant, a summary of your background or a biographical sketch may be attached to the brief but only if it closely relates to the objective.

This format is particularly useful for inexperienced candidates and those with gaps in employment history, because it offers an opportunity to highlight skills acquired in volunteer, academic, recreational, family, or part-time work settings, many of which may be eminently transferable to the particular needs of this employer. (Review Chapters 3, 4, and 5 for identifying, grouping, and naming skills.) Take a look at how one of our clients, Neil, put his qualifications brief together.

Neil F. Thomas
29 Perry Street
San Francisco, CA 94112
415-488-9291

OBJECTIVE

Senior analyst officer position in an investment-management firm of impeccable reputation where the integrity of analysis is as highly valued as the ability to sell the client. Clients will be high-net-worth individuals, organizations, and pension funds that seek to build a market presence based on investment opportunities in foreign countries, particularly in Asia. I seek employment where there is a perceived need for exceptional research and analysis, a conservative approach to risk, an opportunity to grow and manage an autonomous unit, and a spirit of collegial support and cooperation.

QUALIFIED BY

- Recent authorship of two widely acclaimed research books on Asia and South America for a multinational trading firm. As a result of the books' publication, three key clients of the firm have, in the aggregate, tripled their investment activity and, based on my presentations to other clients, we see promise of other increased activity.
- Consultation to the editor of a well-known investment newsletter that resulted in a regular column concentrating in foreign-fund investment.
- Co-leading the establishment of a Malaysian fund at a major U.S. brokerage firm. The fund continues to exist four years following my departure.
- Five years of teaching investment theory at Princeton and Yale universities, during which time I published three major research papers, two of which are now a part of texts in use in most graduate courses in the field.
- PhD dissertation: *The Coming Investment Opportunities in Emerging Asian Economies.*
- Teaching assistantship, Princeton University, in Basic Strategies for a Global Economy.
- Avid participation in debating society for four years, Princeton University.

EDUCATION

- PhD in economics, Princeton University, 1983
- Masters degree in economics, Yale University, 1981
- BS in economics, Princeton University, 1975
- London School of Economics, 1975–76

PERSONAL INFORMATION

Avid reader of German literature; alpine hiker; active participant in choral societies.

Proposal

The best chance you have to convince a current or potential employer that you are the answer to his or her needs is with a proposal. A proposal, first delivered orally and then backed up in writing, demonstrates to the people who have the power to hire you that you have "the right stuff" to do the job. Please consult Chapters 15 and 16 for a complete breakdown of how to assemble on-the-mark proposals.

No matter how simple or how sophisticated your contemplated jobs may seem to you, a proposal will go a long way in convincing decision-makers that they will come out winners if they hire you. Take a look at how Matt, a young, motorcycle-riding, fast-food enthusiast, set up his proposal. He delivered it to the regional manager of a fast-food chain. His proposal worked because he knew what he had to offer and he covered all the items that the manager needed to know. The bracketed headings permit you to follow the structure of his proposal:

MATT'S PROPOSAL

[1. Why I Am Here]

For a long time I have been fascinated with the problems of efficiency in fast-food restaurants. This comes from having earned my way through school by working in cafeterias and concessions. I love good food and I recognize how important speed is to people who have to get back to work. This summer, I toured a three-state region, eating at and closely observing numerous quick-service restaurants. I've come to some conclusions about what may work best with respect to filling customers' orders quickly and courteously.

[2. What I Can Do For You]

What I propose to do for your four restaurants is increase the speed with which customers are served. If your lines move faster than your competitors', your business is likely to increase. I also think I can improve the attitude of your counter staff. (I remember you telling me how discouraged you were with the level of their enthusiasm.) They are very good in comparison with most of your competition, but I believe I can instill in them an extra spirit of enthusiasm.

[3. How I Will Go About It]

I suggest that I start with a single restaurant to show you what I can do. I could work as assistant to the manager, first tackling kitchen efficiency, then counter efficiency and attitude. First of all, I would assess why your kitchen and counter staff are working here, if they enjoy their jobs, how much responsibility they want, and if they would like more varied tasks. Then, based on what I learn, with the manager's approval I would institute simple improvements in procedure or sequence. In this way, the people who have the greatest effect on the customer become instrumental in planning changes. I would need the support of your manager, which I don't think will be a problem, because Joe and I have already talked over these concerns several times. Later I can take my approach to your other locations.

[4. What the Benefits Are for You]

I estimate that you'll see measurable improvements in a month, and in six weeks your lunchtime wait should be cut in half. It is running 20 minutes now, so this means 10 minutes or less. Your manager will be freed up to work on marketing and other matters. I imagine once we take my approach to other locations, you'll be able to deliver on an ad promising "the fastest and best lunch within 20 miles." I also predict you will have less staff turnover.

I am sure I will have some interesting and cost-effective incentive raises to propose for your consideration after I have been on the inside for a while. These will enable you to retain help and keep spirits high. I know you would like to be spending your time scouting out new opportunities rather than putting out fires at your present locations.

[5. Why I Am Qualified]

By this time, you must be thinking, "How does this guy know he can do all of this?" I suppose I'm so sure because I have had lots of opportunity to work with people the same age as your employees. In high school I began working on the cafeteria serving line. The manager pulled me out after three weeks to put me in charge of interviewing and scheduling the kitchen and serving staff. We had a lot of fun that year, and the cafeteria manager hired me back the next two years as his assistant. One summer I was the dining room manager for the YMCA camp at Lake Hiawatha. The next year I was asked back as assistant personnel manager for all camp employees. In college two friends and I opened the first campus all-night diner. We ran it for three years and then sold it to the college. Our success eventually ran away with us. We had some heavy scheduling problems to work out so that we could keep up our grades.

In summary, I'd simply like to say that I hope you can see I'd be a better-than-average bet. Most important, I have come to you before any other quick-service restaurant in the area because I like the quality approach you seem to be aiming for.

[6. Next Step]
Perhaps you would like to talk this over with Joe and then we can meet again. What would you say to next Wednesday? This will give you time to think about the timetable I suggest and the time I would free up for Joe. I'm really very enthusiastic about what we may be able to do together.

Whatever Format You Choose, Make It Look Good

■ Your presentation should always look as though it has been tailor-made for its recipient, which we hope it was. Do not have it professionally printed. Resumes and other written material that look as though they have been sent out by the hundreds will evoke little response.

■ Use action verbs in the present tense. *Did* and *was* suggest that you don't use that skill now. Using "ing" words helps the reader visualize activities as if you were doing them now: *Managing, teaching, selling,* are better choices than *managed, taught,* or *sold.*

■ Center your name, address, telephone number (and fax number, if you have one) at the top.

■ Check and recheck spelling and grammar, and then ask someone else to proofread for you.

■ Limit resumes, curriculum vitaes, biographical sketches, or qualification briefs to two pages.

■ Minimal use of color can be effective if you are using charts or graphs to illustrate points.

■ Use good quality 8½"-x-11" paper.

■ Print it out using a laser or ink jet printer or use a very good quality typewriter (no dot-matrix printers).

■ Skip overly cute design vehicles (no scrolls rolled up in tubes or accordion-pleated fold-outs).

■ No videotapes, audiocassettes, or CD-ROMs unless specifically requested (or unless you are a visual artist making a portfolio).

■ Above all, remember that you—in person—are your own best champion. Learn how to make your contacts in person first, then let your written materials follow.

INDEX

A

Achievements, interview questions
    about, 187
Action verbs, in life stories, 12
Advancement, opportunities for,
    161
Adverbs, in descriptions of skills,
    22
Appreciation, expressing of, 170
Areas of life:
    articulating goals for, 87-88
    categorizing of, 85-86
    relating themes to, 86, 87
Assistants, telephone calls
    intercepted by, 110, 113

B

Background reading, in surveying,
    103, 105, 110, 111, 124,
    179
Benefits (compensation), 161
Benefits to potential employer:
    outlined in proposals, 148-49,
    151
    salary figure justified by, 160-61
"Billboard" exercise, 77-78, 85
    plan of action and, 94
Biographical sketches, 201-2
Body language, in negotiations,
    161
Bonuses, 161
Buyers, as survey contacts, 102

C

Call waiting, 178
Central mission. *See* Goals
Childhood:
    hidden talents from, 10
    referring to events from, 39
Childhood dreams, 64-68, 84
    example of, 64-65
    recalling of, 66-67
    themes in, 80, 84
Chronological resumes, 199-200
Clothes:
    "likes" and "dislikes" lists and,
    53
    for survey meetings, 123
Clubs, as perks, 161
Community environment, 45, 55-
    59
    plan of action and, 94
    refining "likes" and "dislikes"
    lists for, 58-59
Compatibility questions, in inter-
    views, 194-96
Compensation:
    interview questions about,
    196-97
    negotiating of, 152, 157, 158-62
    nonmonetary, 161-62
    see also Salary
Computer databases, on-line
    research and, 179
Consulting work, decision-making
    grid and, 139-41
Co-workers, 45

interview questions about, 196
observing behavior of, 169-70
people values and, 46-52
potential, establishing rapport
  with, 157
Credentials, 43
Curriculum vitae (CV), 200

D

Databases, on-line research and,
  179
Daydreams, 81
Deciding where you want to work,
  131-41
  developing grid or matrix for,
    132-35
  going into business for yourself
    and, 139-41
  matching criteria to choices in,
    137, 140
  numerical ranking for criteria in,
    135-37, 138
  process of, 132
  top five skill clusters and, 134
Describing skills, 19-22
  context in, 20-22
  in interviews, 19-20
Discovering who you are, 1-59
  defining skills and, 19-22
  effectively describing skills and,
    35, 36-40
  life stories and, 9-18, 23-24, 26
  ranking super skills in order of
    enjoyment and competence
    and, 40-43
  skill clusters and, 25-34
  uncovering skills with others
    and, 22-24
  uncovering values and, 45-59
  uncovering your full range of
    skills and, 1-7
"Dislikes" lists:
  for community environment, 55,
    58-59

decision-making grid and,
  134-35
for people, 47, 49, 50, 51-52
plan of action and, 94
for working conditions, 53, 55,
  56
Dreams, 81
  childhood, 64-68, 80, 84

E

Education:
  company benefits and, 161, 162
  to improve super skills high on
    enjoyment list, 43
  interview questions related to,
    191-92
  pursuing old dreams in, 67-68
  specific skills acquired in, 4
Employers, potential:
  addressing needs of, 145,
    147-48, 182, 183
  evaluating of, 137, 140
  identifying of, 120-24
  offering solutions to problems
    of, 145, 148-49
  outlining your potential benefits
    to, 148-49, 151
  research on, 182
  standard interviews with, 181-97
Enthusiasm, expressing of, 170
Expense accounts, 161
Experience, interview questions
  related to, 193-94

F

Fantasies, 81
Fascinations, 69-73
  decision-making grid and, 135
  see also Interests
Firings, interview questions about,
  193-94
Freelance work:

decision-making grid and, 139-41
proposals and, 144
Functional resumes, 200
qualifications briefs, 203-4
Future:
annual review of goals for, 172
continually planning for, 166-67
milestones in, 96
overall game plan for, 167-68
plan of action for, 93-97, 172, 173
"Twenty Years From Now" exercise and, 76-77, 85

G

Goal areas, images for, 86
Goals, 63-90, 173
annual reviews of, 172
"Billboard" exercise and, 77-78, 85
childhood dreams and, 66-68, 84
current interests and, 69-73, 84-85
decision-making grid and, 135
determining what you really want and, 75-81
importance of, 83, 84
incorporating into single statement, 88-90, 95, 135, 180
for individual areas of your life, 87-88
interview questions related to, 189-90
milestones to, 96
"One-Month Adventure" exercise and, 78-80, 85
other people's opinions on, 89
plan of action and, 94-95
quantifiable (objectives), 89
setting of, 83-90
society's "shoulds" and, 75

specificity of, 89
time frame for, 87-88
"Twenty Years From Now" exercise and, 76-77, 85
"What You Want" themes and, 80, 84-86, 87
Grade point average, interview questions about, 191

H

Handshakes, 122
Health insurance, 161
Hobbies, skills associated with, 7
How elements, in life stories, 15, 18

I

Insights, adding to notebook, 93
Interests, 69-73, 84-85
childhood dreams and, 64-68
current, uncovering of, 69, 71-73
decision-making grid and, 135
long-term survival and satisfaction and, 168
money-making opportunities hidden in, 69-71
skills associated with, 7
themes in, 80, 84-85
turning into surveys, 100-106
Interviews, 181-97
clearly describing skills in, 19-20
compatibility questions in, 194-96
compensation questions in, 196-97
education-centered questions in, 191-92
effectively conveying talents in, 36-37
experience-centered questions in, 193-94
goal-centered questions in, 189-90

informational. *See* Survey meetings

information to have in hand for, 184

personal questions in, 185-88

proposal meetings vs., 181

ten steps for, 182-83

traveling to and arriving at, 183

"trick" questions in, 184-85

turning into survey or proposal meetings, 181-82

visualization of, 183

what interviewers are after in, 184

Introductions, 109-15

face-to-face meetings in, 110-11

letters in, 109-11, 113-15

telephone calls in, 109-13

Intuition, 26

J

Job performance, 169-71

appraisals of, 161

enthusiasm and, 170

observing others at work and, 169-70

office systems and, 169

quality and timeliness of work in, 171

surveying for best resources and, 170-71

Jobs:

evaluating offers for, 162-63

negotiating terms of, 155-63

never point of surveying, 107, 122

next, planning for, 166-67

proposals for, 143-53

Job satisfaction:

co-workers and, 45, 46-52

working conditions and, 45, 52-55, 56

L

Layoffs, interview questions about, 193-94

Leisure activities:

money-making opportunities hidden in, 69-71

pursuing old dreams in, 67-68

Letters:

of introduction, 114-15

rules for, 113

to survey contacts, 109-11, 113-15

thank you, 105, 126-27

Life-review sessions, 171

Life stories, 9-18, 39

examples of, 11, 15, 16-17

hidden talents revealed in, 9, 10-13, 18, 23-24, 26

how elements in, 15, 18

organizing thoughts for, 13-14

reading to other people, 23-24

skill clustering and, 26, 30

titling of, 13-14

writing of, 15, 18

"Likes" lists:

for community environment, 55-59

decision-making grid and, 134-35

for people, 46-47, 48, 50, 51

plan of action and, 94

for working conditions, 53-54

Living environment, 45, 55-59

see also Community environment

Long-term survival and satisfaction, 165-73

continually planning for future and, 166-67

job performance and, 169-71

life-review sessions and, 171

overall game plan for, 167-68

plan of action and, 172, 173

reviewing goals and, 172, 173

surveying and, 168, 172

Lunch meetings, 123

M

Meetings:
   with potential co-workers, 157
   see also Interviews; Proposal
      meetings; Survey meetings
Milestones, in plan of action
   poster, 96
Mission statements. *See* Goals
Mrs. Fields Cookies, 10
Moving expenses, 161

N

Needs of potential employer:
   addressing in interviews, 182,
      183
   addressing in proposals, 145,
      147-48
Negotiations, 155-63
   with all of top targets in deci-
      sion-making grid, 158
   on compensation, 152, 157,
      158-62
   first mention of figure in, 160
   object of, 159
   order of issues to discuss in,
      161-62
   practicing for, 159
   reviewing outcome of, 162-63
   signs of getting close to, 156-57
   when to begin, 157
   willingness to walk away from,
      160
   written offers in, 162
Notes from survey meetings, 123, 179

O

Objectives, 89
   see also Goals
Observation, of others at work,
   169-70

Offers:
   evaluating of, 162-63
   negotiating of, 155-63
   written, 162
Office, at home, 177-78
   supplies for, 178
   telephone line in, 178
Office, at work:
   setting up, 169
   working conditions and, 52-55,
      56
"One-Month Adventure" exercise,
   78-80, 85
   plan of action and, 94
Opening statements, in proposals,
   145, 146
Opportunities, surveying for, 120-22
Organization, 177-80
   of office at home, 177-78
   of office at work, 169
   of skills, 25-34; *see also* Skill
      clusters
   of surveys, 179
   of time, 179-80

P

Pensions, 161
People values, 46-52
   decision-making grid and, 134
   plan of action and, 94
Performance. *See* Job performance
Performance-based compensation,
   161
Perks, 161
Personality skills, 5-6, 12
Personal mission. *See* Goals
Personal questions, in interviews,
   185-88
Plan of action, 173
   assembling of, 93-97
   billboard message and, 94
   decision-making grid and, 134
   goals and, 94-95
   likes and dislikes and, 94

one-month adventure and, 94
revising and updating of, 172
super skills and, 94
Plan of action poster, 94-97
discovering links between activities in, 95-96
elements to include in, 94-95
milestones in, 96
survey subject and, 106
Political structure, in workplace, 170
Pressure, interview questions about, 187-88
Problem solving, interview questions about, 188
Promotions, opportunities for, 161
Proposal meetings, 144-53
avoiding compensation discussions during, 152, 157
length of, 153
standard interviews vs., 181
turning standard interviews into, 181-82
Proposals, 143-53, 199
achievements of, 159-60
action steps suggested in, 145, 151
anticipating objections to, 149
charts, pictures, or graphs in, 152
complexity of, 148
evidence offered in support of, 145, 150, 152
of freelancers, 144
importance of, 144-45
long-term survival and satisfaction and, 168
moving to negotiations from, 156-57
needs defined in, 145, 147-48
opening statement in, 145, 146
route to, 144
solutions offered in, 145, 148-49
surveying and, 143, 147, 152
written, 152, 183, 205-8
Providers, as survey contacts, 102

Q

Qualifications briefs, 203-4
Questions:
in interviews, 184-97
in surveying, 103-4, 107, 124-26
Quitting present job:
interview questions about, 194
offers and, 162

R

Raises, 161
Rapport:
with potential co-workers, 157
with survey contacts, 107, 110, 123, 126
Reading:
background, in surveying, 103, 105, 110, 111, 124, 179
clues to interests in, 72
Receptionists, telephone calls intercepted by, 110, 113
Record-keeping, for surveys, 105, 179
References, 194
Relocation, community considerations and, 55-59
Research:
on-line, 179
on salary, 158, 159, 160
see also Surveying
Resources, surveying for, 170-71
Resumes, 199-208
biographical sketches, 201-2
chronological, 199-200
curriculum vitae (CV), 200
functional, 200
presentation of, 207-8
qualifications briefs, 203-4
Role-playing:
before interviews, 182
in survey preparations, 104-5, 106-7, 110, 125

S

Salary:
  employer's criteria and, 158, 159
  interview questions about,
    196-97
  negotiating of, 152, 157, 158-62
  research on, 158, 159, 160
  surveying for information on,
    126
Satisfaction. *See* Job satisfaction;
    Long-term survival and satis-
    faction
Schedules:
  daily, 179-80
  long-term, 180
Scripts, for telephone calls, 110,
    112
Self-knowledge. *See* Discovering
    who you are
"Shoulds," sorting out what you
    really want from, 75
Skill clusters, 25-34, 43-44
  decision-making grid and, 134
  example of, 27-30
  intuitive approach to, 26
  naming of, 27, 31-33, 34
  possible difficulties in, 33
  procedures for, 26-27
  ranking in order of enjoyment
    and competence, 40-43, 134
  refining of, 30
  talking papers and, 37-40, 44
Skills, 184
  basic, or functional, 3
  describing of, 19-22
  discovering of, 1-7
  effectively talking about, 35, 36-40
  hobbies and interests related to, 7
  interview questions about, 193
  organizing of, 25-34
  personality, 5-6, 12
  providing context for, 20-22
  regular life-review sessions and,
    171

revealed in life stories, 9, 10-13,
    18, 23-24, 26
specific, 4
super, 32-33, 34, 35, 37-44, 94
uncovering with other people,
    22
Small businesses, decision-making
    grid and, 139-41
Smoking, 123
Starting your own business, deci-
    sion-making grid and, 139-41
Stock benefits, 161
Super skills, 32-33, 34, 35
  future education and training
    and, 43
  plan of action and, 94
  ranking in order of enjoyment
    and competence, 40-43
  talking papers for, 37-40, 44
Supplies, for home office, 178
Surveying, 99-129
  altering focus of, 119-20
  applicable to all areas of life, 99
  background reading in, 103,
    105, 110, 111, 124, 179
  for best resources at work,
    170-71
  decision-making grid and, 135
  determining subject of, 100, 106
  evaluating what you have
    learned in, 128-29
  in evaluation of offers, 163
  examples of, 100-106, 118-20,
    121, 124-25
  introducing oneself to sources
    in, 105-6, 109-15
  job seeking never point of, 107,
    122
  letters in, 109-11, 113-15
  long-term survival and satisfac-
    tion and, 168, 172
  objective of, 101, 105, 119-20,
    128
  for opportunities, 120-22
  organizing for, 179
  planning for, 105, 106, 128

practicing on topic unrelated to work, 104, 105, 106
preparing questions for, 103-4, 107, 124-26
proposals and, 143, 147, 152
purpose of, 100
record-keeping in, 105, 179
results of, 107
for salary information, 126
sources of information for, 103, 105
telephone calls in, 109-13
thank-you notes in, 105, 126-27
three categories of people to see in, 102
timetable for, 106
turning interest into, 100-106
Survey meetings, 110-11, 122-27, 128
asking good questions in, 124-26
dressing for, 123
establishing rapport in, 123, 126
etiquette for, 122-23
role-playing as practice for, 104-5, 106-7, 110, 125
taking notes or tape recording in, 123
thank-you letters after, 105, 126-27
turning standard interviews into, 181-82

T

Talents. See Skills
Talking about yourself:
effectively conveying your skills and, 35, 36-40
in interviews, 36-37
Talking papers, 37-44
difficulties with, 39
example of, 39-40
interviews and, 182
preparing of, 37-38
proposals supported by

examples from, 150
ranking in order of enjoyment and competence, 40-43, 134
Tape recorders, in meetings, 123
Telephone calls:
best time for, 180
getting beyond receptionist or assistant in, 110, 113
scripts for, 110, 112
to survey sources, 109-13
Telephone line, for home office, 178
Television:
clues to interests in, 72
work environments portrayed in, 54
"Tell me about yourself," as interview question, 185-86
Thank-you letters:
example of, 127
in surveying, 105, 126-27
Themes. See "What You Want" themes
Third parties, as survey contacts, 102, 124
Time, making best use of, 179-80
Timeliness, in job performance, 171
Training, 72
as compensation, 161, 162
to improve super skills high on enjoyment list, 43
specific skills learned in, 4
Travel:
clues to interests in, 72
"One-Month Adventure" exercise and, 78-80, 85
"Twenty Years From Now" exercise, 76-77, 85

U, V

Users, as survey contacts, 102
Values:
community considerations and, 55-59

people, 46-52
uncovering of, 45-59
working conditions and, 52-55,
    56
Voice mail, 178

W, Y

Weaknesses, interview questions
    about, 186-87
"What You Want" themes, 80, 84-
    86
    areas of life identified with, 85-
        86, 87

in childhood dreams, 80, 84
in interests, 80, 84-85
Work environment, 184
    co-workers and, 45, 46-52
    decision-making grid and,
        134-35
    interview questions about, 195
    negotiations and, 161
    observing behavior of others in,
        169-70
    plan of action and, 94
    working conditions and, 45,
        52-55
Yearbooks, clues to childhood
    dreams in, 67